The Neoliberal Undead:

Essays on Contemporary Art and Politics

The Neoliberal Undead:

Essays on Contemporary Art and Politics

Marc James Léger

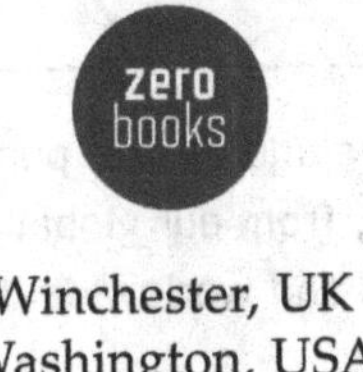

Winchester, UK
Washington, USA

First published by Zero Books, 2013
Zero Books is an imprint of John Hunt Publishing Ltd., Laurel House, Station Approach,
Alresford, Hants, SO24 9JH, UK
office1@jhpbooks.net
www.johnhuntpublishing.com
www.zero-books.net

For distributor details and how to order please visit the 'Ordering' section on our website.

Text copyright: Marc James Léger 2012

ISBN: 978 1 78099 569 4

A CIP catalogue record for this book is available from the British Library.

Design: Stuart Davies

We operate a distinctive and ethical publishing philosophy in all
areas of our business, from our global network of authors to
production and worldwide distribution.

CONTENTS

Acknowledgements

Most of the essays in this book were written between the years 2009 and 2011. I would especially like to thank those individuals who created opportunities for me to present my work, or who helped me sharpen some of the ideas and writing, in particular, Izida Zorde, the Critical Social Research Collaborative at Carleton University, Isabelle Lelarge, Richard Martel, Richard Dyer and Yvie Andrews, Carole Condé and Karl Beveridge, Jackie Sumell and Herman Wallace, Karen van Meenen and Lucia Sommer, Pierre Allard and ATSA, Katy Siegel, Montreal's Convergence des luttes anti-capitalistes (CLAC), Stevphen Shukaitis, Jeff Shantz, Imre Szeman, and Gerald Raunig. Rosika Desnoyers' readings of these essays and my frequent conversations with her helped me to better articulate many of my concerns.

Thanks to all of the artists and cultural institutions that gave me permissions to publish images of artwork and to reprint versions of those essays that have appeared previously. "Art World as Zombie Culture" was first presented in the context of the panel "The Neoliberal Undead: First as Tragedy, Then as Farce," organized by Bruce Barber and myself for the Universities Art Association of Canada Annual Conference, Guelph University, October 2010. Parts of the latter were published in "Whose Excellence? Our Excellence!" *Fuse* 33:3 (Summer 2010) 24-26. "Culture and the Communist Turn" was presented at the *Varieties of Socialism, Varieties of Approaches* conference at Carleton University, March 5, 2011. "Alterglobal Allegory: Condé and Beveridge Against the Commodification of Water," was published in French in *Inter* #107 (Winter 2011) 46-50. "By Any Means Necessary: From the Revolutionary Art of Emory Douglas to the Art Activism of Jackie Sumell" was published in *Afterimage* 38:5 (March/April 2011) 8-14 (See www.vsw.org/ai.).

"Afterthoughts on Engaged Art Practice: ATSA and the State of Emergency," was published in *Art Journal* 70:2 (Summer 2011) 50-65. "The Non-Productive Role of the Artist: The Creative Industries in Canada" was published in *Third Text* 24:5 (September 2010) 50-65. "Protesting Degree Zero: On Black Bloc Tactics, Culture and Building the Movement," was first presented on the *InterActivist Info Exchange* website (November 16, 2010) and subsequently included in Jeff Shantz's edited anthology *Protest and Punishment*. "The Québec Maple Spring, the Red Square and After" was presented on the website of the European Institute for Progressive Cultural Policy in October 2012.

Some mention should be made also of the people who are involved in the radical reshaping of contemporary art discourse and with whom I have had the pleasure of working or discussing. Among them are Brian Holmes, Gregory Sholette, Jennifer Gradecki, Michael Blum and Barbara Clausen, Oliver Ressler, David Tomas, Claude Lacroix as well as Jason Jones, Beka Economopulos and Jodi Dean at Not An Alternative. Special thanks go to Tariq Goddard and John Hunt at Zero Books, and Marc Herbst at the *Journal of Aesthetics and Protest*. For financial assistance I wish to acknowledge the Government of Québec. Superlatives are reserved for Cayley Sorochan, champion of ideology critique, and special dedications go to my father, Thomas Léger, who taught me how to spot a zombie.

Introduction

Marc Herbst

Institutional critique is conservative; its function is either as house-cleaning or as rearguard action. Instead, Marc Léger's work appears energized by its continuing commitment to keep central the potential to create change with art as one tool. Radical writing is done at the point where criticized institutions meet (facilitate and/or negate) the potentials for artwork. Marc Léger's work hangs out at *this* spot.

To many, revolution has a relationship to art and its institutions. In that relationship, the institution is secondary and appears as tertiary. Few culture-rads tune their dials to the music of the non-profit board. Instead, they choose to vibe with the art and music. But no matter, when the music fades and the art is taken down, it is the institution that remains. That is what institutions do.

Much contemporary writing tends to ignore this. Instead, it is often hung up on the singular artists. I like Marc James Léger's work because he understands this and suffers no delusions for art.

Revolution year zero only exists within an exhibition. To know this is important.

Many assume that each work of art is singular, an isolated existential phenomenon. Many encounter political artwork as a radical island that formed from the viewer's discovery. But there is no revolution year zero. Instead, waves of to-be-formed revolutionaries wash through and encounter both ancient and new archipelagos of institutions whose bedrock is formed from sedimented compositions, common knowledges, and collective procedures. Between palm trees, the islands' bookshelves are stuffed with new and old books, posters, images, culture, landscapes, architectures, holidays, songs, sculptures, stories, laws. These bookshelves are open and their contents can be carried away. It is for the young and newly radical to make something of this detritus, however they find it. However, the common knowledge, collective procedures, and compositions are held more tightly.

Knowing this, some of Léger's keenest critiques are held out for relational aesthetics and social practice. He describes these trends as being thin deep and a mile wide. Though the *Journal of Aesthetics & Protest* (which I co-edit) has published several of his critical essays on these topics, his work managed to make us sweat under our colours.

At its inception, our magazine rallied against those who would complicate our ideal of the artist as revolutionary by, among other things, bringing boring questions about museum and gallery art into the picture. For my part, as an editor, I built my perspective on 90s counterculture. I dug through the trash at the Kinkos on Houston Street to claim the discards from Seth Tobacman and Eric Drooker's zine-making forays. Based on such discards, I assumed that there would be both a residue of freedom-from-work and a how-to-manual for an artistic revolution. I dug the 90s for what it could distinctly offer. Imagine now that thin post-Cold War moment with digital technology and counter-historic culture's ungentrified neighborhoods: pirate radio, video freaks, tech hackers, community gardens, and the anarchist bookstore – projects that a decade later would be re-created as social practice and relational aesthetics.

Staring down the rabbit hole of an ever-more structurally precarious economy, art appeared to me in the 90s not as a grouping of flawed institutions but rather as a container for unified identity. Drooker and Tobacman were people, people who danced, people who were committed to the community gardens and the historic legacies of the Lower East Side through the stories they told, the people they knew and the songs they sang. They were not employees of an art scene but individual actors. Their art seemed to have permission and to be extra-institutional. They got things done, carried their own stuff. But upon starting our Journal, my reference was wrong. I had assumed that underground artwork was synonymous with fine art. It is not.

The last decade has been a decade of intense neoliberalization. The art industry has deeply infiltrated culture. Institutions stand. The museum has expanded and resists my efforts to communalize society. Our Journal *now* wrestles with this reality. With his consistently sharp talons, Marc Léger has helped us do so.

Léger is the first art critic I've liked. The angry undercurrent *I've* read in his pointed critiques led me to assume he was an autodidact (his bio said "independent scholar"). I was wrong. He has a PhD. I count him among the select group of PhDs smart enough to have taken the time to learn how to intelligently eviscerate the load of bullshit they encounter within the institutions we all must tangle with.

As abstract machines or as really brick-and-mortar we must tangle with institutions. Affirmatively, as an activist, I've witnessed how NGOs like Rainforest Action Network and the Steelworkers Union can be an important component of a movement much broader than themselves.

I often wonder what it would be like to encounter what I know as a solidified landscape. I imagine a neighbourhood somewhere that embodies my social, historical and critical perspectives in its public holidays, school board, cultural center, courts, clubs and street signs, lamp posts, litter boxes and stores. I imagine this as a place in process and integrated within the normal fabric of a much larger society (otherwise it'd be very lame). I wonder what it would be to walk these streets as a teenager, to move in and decide to call this place home. What would it be like to be organically informed by this knowledge as physical structures? How would it go to launch a radical cultural practice from here?

It would be lame for me to say that in this neighborhood, Marc Léger's critical insights would be reflected in the finest buildings' facades (in this neighborhood, the finest buildings might be reserved for the kindergarten, head shop and culture centre). Instead, I'll say that his thoughts would be scrawled (in permanent chalk) near the gutters. Lost teens and twenty-somethings would walk past these thoughts on their way to the liberated cultural centre. While enjoying the show, they also might hang out on the corner, appreciating how the whole thing comes together, and grumble just a bit. They would grumble about the fact that despite the brick and mortar there's a continued potential for something different, elsewhere and here. The kids see what bullshit the whole thing is. It's not a bad attitude; instead it helps them understand what they aren't seeing and why.

Art World as Zombie Culture: Excellence, Exodus and Ideology

It's a modern folly to alter the corrupt ethical system, its constitution and legislation, without changing the religion, to have a revolution without a reformation.
– G.W.F. Hegel

What they do not recognize is that twenty-first century capitalism as a whole is a zombie system, seemingly dead when it comes to achieving human goals and responding to human feelings, but capable of sudden spurts of activity that cause chaos all around.
– Chris Harman

In March of 2010, a large number of artists, curators and cultural workers from Canada and abroad added their names to an open letter addressed to Marc Mayer, Director of the National Gallery of Canada, for a series of comments he made during a CBC report on diaspora art and the cultural politics of public institutions.[1] Mayer's comments to reporter Jelena Adzic can be summarized with the following quote: "Our real mandate is excellence. We do think about diversity, however... We put on what we find in the Canadian art scene that is excellent and we're blind to colour or ethnic background, or even whether you were born in Canada, we don't care. (...) We're looking for excellent art. We don't care who makes it." Mayer's words echo those of John Lydon in the 2008 Country Life butter television commercial: "Do I buy Country Life butter because it's British? No. I buy Country Life because I think it tastes the best." All the while Lydon is metaphorically wrapped in the British flag and is surrounded by the trappings of the stereotypical British upper class. In the *Eighteenth Brumaire*, Karl Marx famously stated that "the great events and characters of world history occur twice; first as tragedy, then as farce." In his reading of these lines in the context of the global economic meltdown and trillion dollar bailouts of 2008-2009, Slavoj Žižek remarks that Herbert Marcuse added to this Marxist reading of Hegel the fact that in some ways, the farce can be more terrifying than the original tragedy.[2]

If such a sequence applies in this case, it is not so much Mayer's cavalier posturing that is laughable, but the reactions to it. Mayer's statements solicited the organized response of people who gathered first through email, then through the social networking site Facebook, and then posted as an online blog called excellenceatthenationalgallery.[3] The open letter, penned by curators Milena Placentile and Emily Falvey, and with the subsequent support of curator Ryan Rice, quickly became a catalyst for scrutiny of the NGC's mandate and policies. The letter takes exception with Mayer's comments, which seem to ignore recent efforts on the part of the NGC to address its colonial legacy. It states:

> This begs the question: Whose excellence? This is what women and ethnic minorities have been asking for centuries. (...) Today you tell us that [the] NGC doesn't show ethnic minorities because they are not achieving 'excellence.' The simplistic notion that connoisseurs know 'good art' was thoroughly discredited by twentieth-century feminist and post-colonial writers, artists and activists... Well, we know 'excellence' when we see it, and today we prefer to call it hegemony.

The letter goes on to recommend to Mayer some essential reading from feminist art historian Linda Nochlin, post-colonial theorist Edward Said, African-American cultural theorist bell hooks and some familiarity with *Fuse* Magazine.[4]

The intellectual background to the letter, as I interpreted it, amounts to something that approaches the radical democracy that was proposed by Ernesto Laclau and Chantal Mouffe in their 1985 book *Hegemony and Socialist Strategy: Towards a Radical Democratic Politics*.[5] Among the many arguments put forward in this book is the concept of *equivalence* – a concept that presupposes an equivalence among different kinds of struggle against oppression, be it based on race, class, gender or sexuality. On this "multicultural" basis, the idea of a value-free notion of excellence does appear ridiculous, or at least quixotic. To take up Žižek's inquiry in *First as Tragedy, Then as Farce*, we could ask the question: What is the link not only between the liberal technocracy of major cultural institutions like the National Gallery but between the identity politics proposed in the letter and today's dominant ideological view that communism is no longer a pertinent tool of analysis, nor a viable political alternative, and that nothing should stand in the way of the emergence of a new global class of superrich who accept as a calculated risk the wild speculation that led from dotcom crash in the early 2000s to investments in mortgage schemes that were destined to fail? Further, what do we in the art world have to do with the rise of populist conservatism and the avoidance of the consequences of such liberal-democratic blackmail?[6] Today's discursive "anti-essentialist" historicism, Žižek argues, "views every social-ideological entity as the product of a contingent struggle for hegemony".[7] The problem with today's academic social constructionism, he continues, is that

> this universalized historicism has a strange ahistorical flavor: once we accept and practice the radical contingency of our identities, all authentic historical tension somehow evaporates in the endless performative games of an eternal present. There is a nice self-referential irony at work here: there is history only insofar as there persist remainders of "ahistorical" essentialism. This is why radical anti-essen-

tialists have to deploy all their hermeneutic-deconstructive skills to detect hidden traces of "essentialism" in what appears to be a postmodern "risk society" of contingencies – were they to admit that we already live in an "anti-essentialist" society, they would have to confront the truly difficult question of the historical character of today's predominant radical historicism itself, i.e., confront the topic of this historicism as the ideological form of "postmodern" global capitalism.[8]

We could say, then, to extend Žižek's analysis, that for the utopian form of the ideology of capitalism, counter-hegemonic identity politics and post-structuralist social constructionism act as the utopian ideology of the progressive art world.

In the work of some of the most sophisticated thinkers of our day there is a critique of just such post-politics – the view that the major political struggles and "meta discourses" of the nineteenth and twentieth centuries are a thing of the past and that we must now turn to the endless plurality of *petites histoires*, micropractices and the multitude of singularities. In today's global capitalism, Žižek argues, particular interests are not only universalized by hegemonic forces, but, more to the point, we become universal for ourselves. The way that we come to relate to ourselves in modernity and postmodernity is as people with specific identities and stories to tell, in a way, hoping that these narratives, instead of a grand displacement of the system of cultural production, will become a means of cultural contestation. In liberal capitalist ideology, however, identity also coincides with the ruthless measuring of value in terms of the universal market forces of global capitalism. For these reasons, we should not only consider our collective cultural wealth as such, but should attempt to draw the links between this cultural commons and the social commons by asserting the struggle against capitalism.[9] Here, a further demand imposes itself: the demand for artists and activist collectives to put forward social solutions to the destructive effects of capitalism. Rather than fight the ideology of capitalism head on, we are compelled, in the absence of a strong welfare state, to fight its consequences. Those eager to do well in the system, however, dedicate themselves pointlessly to rebuilding the otiose and decrepit middle class. If 1989 represents the beginnings of the Fukuyaman dream of the "end of ideology," the response to 9/11 and the 2008 meltdown are two good reasons why capitalism deserves a 1989 of its own.

The problem with the very possibility of reimagining class struggle today, as the cultural theorist Brian Holmes argues, is the "absence of any coordinated oppositional force."[10] Because of this, what he proposes for radical cultural practice is an exodus from the museum-magazine-gallery system.[11] Exodus, he writes, "is an expression of process politics. It points beyond the distorting mediations and structural inequalities of capitalism towards a strange sort of promised land for the profane, which is the immediacy of the everyday, the direct experience of cooperation with others."[12] This concept of exodus is derived from the struggles in the 1970s of the Italian autonomist movement in which workers determined to escape both the control of factory managers and communist party directives. In more recent times, it has inspired the 1998 Days of Action in Europe, the Direct Action Network's coordination of protests in Seattle in 1999, and the Euro Mayday protests organized around the struggles of precarious workers such as the Milanese Chainworkers and the French *Intermittents du spectacle*. One of its methods of organizing, according to Holmes, and as indicated in the title of his book, is the collective phantom. Collective phantoms include multiple names like Monty Cantsin, Luther Blisset or Tute Bianche, Reclaim the Streets, The Yes Men, Ya Basta!, No One Is Illegal or even the Zapatistas. Multiple names like these, he writes,

> bring the refusal of copyright and intellectual property to the very center of ego-dominated subjectivity, in an attempt to dissolve the proprietary function of the signature which has always served as the barrier between contemplative, individualistic art and collective, interactive forms of expression.[13]

Through such methods as collective phantoms, new cartographies, tactical media and over-identification pranks, Holmes argues that cultural producers can avoid the alienation of unique signatures and the fetishization of art objects and art experiences via the machinery of institutional art exhibitions.

Holmes' reflections make one wonder what it is that artists want or expect from institutions like the National Gallery. The kinds of radical art practices that Holmes discusses have more in common with 1960s and 70s strategies of anti-institutional contestation than postmodern strategies of complicity and representation. The signatories of the letter would seem in comparison to be rather like the zombies in George Romero's 1978 horror film *Dawn of the Dead*, a film that takes place in a Pittsburgh shopping mall. What do the zombies want with a shopping mall, asks one of the last remaining humans. Another answers: "This was an important place in their lives."

On this theme, I want to make a series of observations that may or may not add up to a practical suggestion for those like Holmes, Gerald Raunig and Paolo Virno who are willing to follow Moses to the promised land. The Deleuzian presuppositions of Holmes' use of the theme of exodus is decidedly antidialectical, refusing the ostensible return to the same via the clash of opposites.[14] The publisher of Holmes' book, *Unleashing the Collective Phantoms*, is Autonomedia, a press that is well-known for its texts that are left of the left. The title of his book is inspired in part by a website that is associated with the work of the Association of Autonomous Astronauts – not a bad reference point for the brave couple that flies away from the zombie mall at the end of *Dawn of the Dead*. "We are not interested in going into space to be a vanguard of the coming revolution," writes Ricardo Balli. Rather, the AAA are involved in virtual class struggle via collective phantoms.[15]

One such phantom, also cited by Holmes, is Boris Karloff, author of the tract "Resisting Zombie Culture." In this text, Karloff attempts to hypnotize her readers by enumerating five different anti-zombification techniques: (1) Collective Phantoms: multiple names that discard individual identities and use multiple imaginations to fabricate and disseminate cultural projects; (2) Media Invasions: tactical projects that use the power of the last remaining humans to reverse the zombification function of the various media machines; (3) Speculative Playgrounds: spaces that are created for the sake of epistemological games; (4) Psychogeographical Tours: wanderings that reclaim the "free" time that is stolen from humans by the work and consumer routines of Zombie Culture; (5) Funk Themes: memes and the like that operate beyond verbal comprehension, and therefore elude capture by the manipulation of Zombie Culture.[16] For the sake of definition, Karloff explains that Zombie Culture is "an elaborate program of mind invasion supervised by Vampire Management." It "aims at implanting specific forms of ideology into our minds ... to ensure that zombies are sufficiently diverted from pursuing liberatory projects." If anti-zombie behaviour is an imminent force in everyone, Karloff adds, why is it then that so many people want to be zombies? Clearly, judging by the number of signatories of the excellenceatthenationalgallery petition letter, they're dying to get in. This is indeed a frightening situation since these zombies are not the slow-moving, funny zombies of the early Romero films, but the quick, weapon-wielding, flying, and severed-skull type Nazi zombies weaned on the blood and bile of post-structuralism, discourse theory and difference politics.

In his account of German Idealism, with its fascination with vampires and the living dead, Žižek argues that the best account of zombies is provided by Immanuel Kant, who, in his *Critique of Pure Reason*, distinguishes between a negative judgement and an infinite judgement.[17] With a negative judgement, you are *not* dead – therefore you are alive. No problem. With an infinite judgement, you are *undead*; you are alive but as dead. Infinite judgement opens up a third unforeseen domain of some obscene word beyond life and death, an excess that culture attempts to cope with. Žižek asserts this third domain against thinkers like Gilles Deleuze who argue that dialectics impose a return to the same through the non-differential "synthesis." In a historical framework, no such return is possible. This expels from Žižek's account both the dogmatism of historical materialism and simplistic critiques of teleology. The truth of most zombie films is that as fictions they attempt to cope with the denaturalizing processes of late capitalism, and every new zombie film addresses a different historical conjuncture. The problem then is that once you admit that you are in a zombie movie, you retroactively de-naturalize nature, and in our case, we de-naturalize cultural production to reveal the international art market and global tourism. The choice between dying a death at the hands of institutional autonomy and dying a death at the hands of the global creative industries is thus a matter of surplus enjoyment, a scenario that is encountered by the cultural worker as an element of fantasy. In this sense, a collective phantom is designed to accept the worst outcome, but in a way that alters the nature of the fantasy and its real-world, symbolic outcomes.

We could, however, question some of Holmes' assumptions about activist art ("class struggle as artistic experience") as an art that is premised on non-economic values such as: a withdrawal from salaried labour; a technological communications commons; file sharing, free software, open-source technology, peer-to-peer exchange and networked intelligence; general nomadism; semiotic economy; pre-individual indistinction; networked collaboration as a high-tech gift economy. I would make the Marxist observation that in a world that is dominated by exchange values, in which people buy and sell commodities and services, in which people have to sell their labour in order to survive, and in which non-productive semiotic labour is mediated by the productive labour of an increasingly proletarianized Third World, use values are intrinsically mediated by exchange values. Use value has no existence apart from its commodity status. Despite this, I would insist also with Marx that quality and the sensuous particularity of people and things are independent of the cash nexus and the relations of exchange. It is through the very quality of people and things, however, that value is expressed in terms of quantities. Calculation and cooperation are thus not merely the behavioural presupposition of the flexible personality within neoliberal societies of risk and control, but the essence of the capitalist relations of production.

From here we could make an important observation concerning cultural production and that is the fact that, as Janet Wolff explains, art as we know it makes its appearance along with the rise of industrial production and bourgeois ideology.[18] The social and economic production of art values has thus depended on various institutions, including educational institutions, universities, academies, and forms of patronage – from the state to individual consumers, audiences, critics, publishers, galleries, media companies, and so on. Anti-zombification techniques do no so much change these aspects of the social production of art, but provide a set of alternatives in a process of differentiation. Today's socially engaged art activism is in this sense quite similar in its ideology and modus operandi to the development of a sphere of bohemian cultural autonomy in the nineteenth century. Of course in today's activist art the development of a field of aesthetic autonomy as a bulwark against bourgeois utilitarianism and gross materialism has been completely reversed and a good deal of art activism, much like the institutionalized labour parties, is oriented towards reform rather than revolution. To use the terminology developed by Peter Bürger in *Theory of the Avant-Garde*, I would argue that the political practices of today's networked activists often correspond to the habitus of a contemporary transnational bohemia that is haunted by the successes and strategies of the revolutionary "historical" avant-gardes.[19]

According to Žižek, the relation between necessity and contingency in Hegel is non-dialectical. Necessity realizes itself in contingency, not in a foregone conclusion or in a behavioural matrix. In this way, the present contains the past and the past gains possibility, or virtuality, as influence. The past is constantly, retroactively reconstructed. At every historical point, he argues, we live in a totality that is necessary in a contingent way and that is retroactively reconstructed. The epistemological limit is that reality itself is incomplete. One problem that faces today's networked art activists is the way in which practice attempts to quickly fill in the gap posed by this symbolic impossibility and thereby conforms to the position of the hysteric who seeks to positivize the place of the big Other. What we get with exodus, I would argue in this Lacanian-Žižekian sense, is a politics that does not want to pay the price for politics. Schizo-anarchists would no doubt agree, referring to anti-zombification strategies as post-political micro-politics. The quest of today's counter-cultural activists would seem to be the effort to localize the antagonism of social difference in a distinction between us (humans) and them (zombies) that falsely universalizes the social antagonism itself. What we get, at best, is not the ideal of socialism or communism but the pragmatism of libertarianism and the populist pluralism of social democracy. In a zombie world the inside and the outside become indistinct, the cultural super-structure is collapsed into the post-Fordist base and the mediating operations of ideology are presumed to have vanished into thin air.

In his 1996 publication, *The University in Ruins*, Bill Readings argued that the kind of cultural nationalism that was once characteristic of institutions like the National Gallery of Canada has been replaced by the technocratic management of a transnational class of people who refuse identification with a specific class status or cultural identity.[20] The idea of universal cultural standards that are the object of feminist and postcolonial critique may not refer to the same markers of excellence that actually form the basis of cultural administration in places like the NGC, even if at times its executives rely on atavistic intellectual frameworks. Excellence, as Readings describes it, has less to do with the formal criteria of evaluation – or even political criteria – than with performance indicators that directly link intellectual and creative production to a global marketplace within which national institutions operate as cultural brokers. Excellence in this regard is not only concerned with markers of identity; it regulates and manages cultural differences in favour of market-based notions of human and cultural capital that are themselves tied to biopolitical state regulation.

Almost anyone who has been taught critical cultural theories in undergraduate and graduate university programmes understands that as soon as you put forward a class analysis of culture and relate culture to its socioeconomic conditions of production you run the risk of being charged with "economism," "reflectionism," or "vulgar Marxism." For some, this is enough to leave behind all sociology and move on to more exciting cultural analysis. Wolff argues that sociologists, in wanting to expose the social bases of aesthetic judgement and taste, tend to discredit aesthetics altogether. She argues against this kind of "sociological imperialism" as well as its flipside, "postmodern relativism," and holds that one cannot indefinitely remain an "agnostic" and forever postpone aesthetic choices.[21] In other words, we all eventually make judgements concerning cultural excellence, even though we may not expect these judgements to be universally valid.[22]

There is a supplement to Wolff's argument against agnosticism, however, in Žižek's theory of belief.[23] Parents do not believe in Santa Claus, he explains, but in their ritualistic actions, and through their children, they effectively believe anyway. The children relieve the parents of the burden of believing. In some ways, this is the work that museum directors, curators and other cultural administrators perform for national and international publics. The NGC's constituents, in this instance, are relieved of the burden to believe in universal aesthetic criteria, or of having to define some for themselves, as long as there are gatekeepers within institutions who are willing to perform this task for them. This at least goes some way in explaining the profoundly social nature of all cultural meaning. Another word for belief in Žižek's writing is ideology. The NGC could very well do more in terms of equity and yet nevertheless continue to operate as an institution that serves the neoliberal "end of ideology" status quo. The same is true of cultural production at all levels, from art schools to artist-run centres. There is therefore some real validity to Holmes' critique of the museum-magazine-gallery system as even alternative institutions show signs of acquiescence to the fetishism of community and creativity.

This brings me to the *faux pas* made by Adzic in her news report, wherein she conflated diaspora art and work by artists of colour with "outsider art" – a category usually reserved for art made by children, the insane, folk artists or sometimes by artists who are unaware of modernist cultural frameworks. Perhaps the real outsider art is art that through its manifest content represents an outside to capitalism. This art would have to be, within the social totality, the art of those who resist the reduction of life and all human culture to the workings of free market ideology.

Culture and the Communist Turn

The Arab Spring of 2011 and the ouster of authoritarian leaders in Tunisia and Egypt have been hailed as instances of revolutionary uprising. No sooner had these brief victories been celebrated, a host of setbacks have beset radical efforts in Yemen, Saudi Arabia, Algeria, Morocco, Jordan, Syria and Libya. Even in Egypt, as early as March of 2011, the interim government sought to reimpose restrictions on the right to publicly demonstrate and the international economic community sought to restabilize the Egyptian economy so that it could better control it from abroad. The contours of socialist uprising against unemployment and austerity, echoed faintly in the United States in Wisconsin, Michigan and Ohio, have been seen to be everywhere conditioned by technocratic political management. Some resist calling these events revolutions, however. Theorists Michael Hardt and Antonio Negri argue that these events resemble rather the anti-globalization movements that since Seattle, Genoa, Buenos Aires and Cochabamba have operated as a leaderless multitude that consolidates demands through a constituent process, a new form of expression represented by network relations.[1] The same events have been received by socialist party organizations worldwide as instances of worker solidarity and have been said to underscore the long-term efforts of working-class trade unions. According to Anne Alexander, the Egyptian revolts, caused by global economic crisis, were preceded by the 2003 demonstrations, the 2006 strike wave and 2008 youth activism. The Egyptian revolution, she argues, demonstrates the grass-roots organizational power of the working class.[2]

At the 2011 conference organized by the Critical Social Research Collaborative, titled "Varieties of Socialism, Varieties of Approaches," the question of multitude versus proletariat was made problematic due to the relative absence of women participants. Gulden Ozcan and Priscilla Lefebvre raised this issue in the lunchtime plenary, "Radical Feminism, Anti-Racism & Socialism: Challenges and Opportunities."[3] My own presentation, "The Political Implications of Contemporary Socially Engaged Art," raised this question of debates between "utopian" and "scientific" socialism through a brief examination of the 2010 Creative Time Summit.[4] In the following I offer a more detailed presentation of the emerging potential for a shift from anti-globalization protest toward communist organization. I add to this some thoughts concerning the contradictions of contemporary socially engaged art.

Globalization

It is generally agreed that the anti, alter or other-globalization movement originated in the late 1990s in the context of protests against the meetings of the World Trade Organization in Seattle and at subsequent protests against G8 and G20 summits. The World Trade Organization, the World Bank and the International Monetary Fund are United Nations institutions that emerged after World War II with an agenda of privatization directed squarely against the nationalization of industry and political sovereignty. The social and economic policies of these institutions were designed to serve the interests of multinational and transnational corporations. In their efforts to protect capitalists, investors and shareholders against social regulation, the function of these institutions has resulted in the entrenchment of right wing politics. The anti-globalization movement represents the collective efforts of social democrats, socialists, anarchists and communists to confront the resulting criminalization of left-wing politics.

According to Maude Barlow and Tony Clark's 2001 book, *Global Showdown*, the WTO enforces international trade agreements that work to consolidate the power of wealthy corporations over and against poor countries.[5] Agreements like GATT

(General Agreement on Trade and Tarifs), GATS (General Agreement on Trade in Services), TRIPS (Trade Related Intellectual Property Measures), TRIMS (Trade Related Intellectual Property Measures), FSA (Financial Services Agreement), AOA (Agreement on Agriculture), ASCM (Agreement on Subsidies and Countervailing Measures), Agreement on TBT (Technical Barriers to Trade), and AGP (Agreement on Government Procurement) enforce international fiscal, social and environmental rules, patents, copyrights and trademarks that prevent poor countries from having cheap access to various necessities, from food to medicines. Trade laws force governments to give private corporations unregulated access to markets, allowing the free movement of capital and simultaneously imposing regressive measures affecting labour laws, safety regulations and environmental protections.

As a legal entity with international status, the WTO allows countries to legally challenge other countries on behalf of corporate clients, bypassing the advice and expertise of local agencies. WTO tribunals are able to strike down state laws, thereby undermining the representative power of democratically elected governments. These UN economic institutions represent the interests of global capitalism over and against all claims made by state governments to democratic law. While WTO officials are in no way accountable to any state government, they work to pass laws that require the assent of all WTO members, with special authority given to the United States, Japan, Canada and the European Union. Corporations have unique access to WTO officials and are backed by well-funded think tanks and corporate lobbyists. Despite that fact that most WTO, WB and IMF decisions work against the UN Declaration of Human Rights, by threatening the environment, food safety, social security, international peace, public education and public health, and despite the fact that they contribute to economic decline in developing countries, they continue to operate internationally through the consent of the silent majority, the power of the state, and the machinations of the powerful.

In the area of cultural production, globalization has worked through free trade agreements to construe culture as a commodity that is subject to forms of appropriation by private capital. Whereas culture was once associated with national identity, with local traditions, communities and forms of solidarity, under neoliberalism culture begins to operate as an adjunct of capitalism with a human, transnational face. In the form of diversity in particular, culture is construed by development agencies as a means to obfuscate class difference and income disparity. Defined in terms of market value and as intellectual property, art is treated in the same terms as seed varieties or medicines, with patents and copyright protections obviating collective rights. This favours the construal of culture in terms of commercial entertainment or as tourism and heritage, which are seen as means to develop economies through export and through import substitution. According to George Yúdice, this view of culture as a source of economic growth is accompanied and legitimized by a view of culture as simultaneously solving the problems created by neoliberalization's negative social effects.[6] Culture becomes another means through which populations are managed. People are in fact encouraged to assert their identities in this context, which can be managed as a resource and which can be used to promote corporate-oriented exchange. Sociopolitical ameliorism thus corresponds to the immaterialization of labour as a new source of economic potential. The contradiction is of course that the corporate promotion of multicultural tolerance and community services is almost a direct outcome of the dramatic subjection of regions and neighbourhoods to commercial imperatives, with the resulting reduction of employment and social services. In this context, artists and activists unwittingly become the "willing executioners" of public management and development experts whose main concern is that culture produce a return on investment.

Proletarianization

A great deal of discussion in Western nations has been focused on the precarization of labour that has accompanied globalization and the shift towards a post-industrial economy. Beginning in the late 1970s and as part of the reaction of New Right governments to welfarism, public institutions were brutally restructured so that they could ostensibly "survive" economically in the global marketplace. Increasing the power of centralized authority, neoliberal governments oversaw a shift from manufacturing to a service economy, creating an unstable employment structure with growth in the consumption of various kinds of services. As a result, a flexible, skilled and educated workforce has become a permanent feature of the new economy. Despite the fact that most of this workforce faces unstable working conditions in part-time and low-skilled service jobs, there has been a great deal of optimism with regard to its class composition. This class of workers tends, like the salaried petty bourgeois classes of old, to not think of itself in class terms, but rather to emphasize identity markers. Variously described as the multitude or the pracariat, and with its specialization in immaterial, flexible and creative labour, the standard line is that this is not the traditional, white, male, blue-collar industrial proletariat, but rather the next generation to follow in the path of the New Left, with its variety of single issues and lifestyle concerns.

The background to this "postmodernization" of politics cannot be limited to the appearance of civil rights, second wave feminism, gay liberation, and consumer and environmental politics, however. A more systematic factor is the global recession that began at the end of 1973 and the shift in economic policies away from welfare state interventions towards monetarist policies. Around this time, unemployment began to be accepted as a natural constraint, even by labour parties, and neoconservatives gave themselves the task of breaking trade union monopolies. For more than one reason, the politically correct 1980s were not a good time to be working-class (male or female), and so conversion strategies became the means to make politics *culturally* relevant. Multiculturalism, identity politics and performative embodiment became the watchwords of "new times" cultural studies. Postmodernist scholars declared the end of Marx and Freud and along with them, anything remotely approaching revolutionary left politics. The current success of post-Fordist theory and the reign of the new communication technologies should perhaps be cause enough to remind us of the social, cultural and political contexts in which economic globalization became the dominant mode of production. In *Zombie Capitalism*, the late Chris Harman argues that by the 1980s, capitalism was coming up against the limits of both monetarism and Keynesianism.[7] With a forty percent reduction of industrial production worldwide, global competition and the race to produce resulted in the closing of plants and the firing of workers. Deepening stagnation continued despite increased arms expenditures and a competitive word system became the precondition for the new economic ideology of neoliberalism. The "Washington Consensus," as it came to be known, was marked by the institutionalization of the IMF and the WB as keystones to global structural adjustment programs that allowed fast capital to be invested in foreign markets with increasingly few trade restrictions. Gaps increased between the rulers and the ruled, Harman says, with high levels of corruption becoming the norm rather than the exception.[8]

Harman asks us to consider what forces are capable of revolting against the current runaway system, with its economic crises and wars. The working class, he argues, because of its place in the mode of production, has the most potential to achieve reforms. For this, however, it must overcome unevenness in the workplace, geographically, and in terms of the divisions of skill and pay. Harman argues that in contemporary theory the dismissal of the working class as a revolutionary agency has been widely accepted. The presupposition he discredits is the one that assumes that the working class belongs to the past and that the future will be overwhelmingly middle-class. The fashionable sociology of Laclau and Mouffe's *Hegemony and Socialist Strategy* and Hardt and Negri's *Empire*, he argues, "departs from empirical reality."[9] Statistics for the 1990s indicate that the middle class represents only ten percent of the 2.5 billion wage workers of the world. Its function is by and large to help control the mass of workers. "Anyone who believes we have said 'fairwell' to this [working] class," he writes, "is not living in the real world."[10] With a core of two billion people and a third of the global population, the working class is the majority of the population, he says, for the *first* time in history. In the U.S. alone, the working class was twenty percent larger in the late 1990s than it was in the early 1970s, and fifty percent larger than in the 1950s. Industrial production in the U.S. was eight percent higher in 2007 than in 2000 and thirty percent higher than in 1996. Negri's Italy, Harman says, does not have the same class composition as the U.S. and Japan, where industry and manufacturing continue to play a greater role than services. Moreover, jobs that were once defined as blue-collar are today classified as white-collar service jobs. Regardless of all of the hype about a post-industrial, post-Fordist economy, most service employees are manual workers. In the U.S., service employees who do manual work represent seventy-five percent of the country's workforce.

Harman goes so far in *Zombie Capitalism* as to suggest that the concept of precarity is in fact overemphasized by capitalists in order to demoralize workers.[11] István Mészáros echoes Harman when he writes:

Just think of the once sharply stressed distinction between

"white-collar" and "blue-collar" workers. As you know, the propagandists of the capital system who dominate the cultural and intellectual processes like to use the distinction between the two as yet another refutation of Marx, arguing that in our societies blue-collar manual work altogether disappears, and the white-collar workers, who are supposed to enjoy a much greater job security (which happens to be a complete fiction), are completely elevated into the middle classes (another fiction). Well, I would say even about the postulated disappearance of blue-collar work: hold on, not so fast! For if you look around the world and focus on the crucial category of the "totality of labor," you find that the overwhelming majority of labor still remains what you might describe as blue-collar. In this respect it is enough to think of the hundreds of millions of blue-collar workers in India, for instance.[12]

The issue, according to Mészáros, is not whether the working class is the sole agency of change, but rather that proletarianization names the process that occurs in the capitalist system.[13] Under capitalism, he argues, the majority of people lose control of the conditions that affect their lives. Control of social reproduction leads proletarians to have some limited autonomy but to be mostly powerless. For Mészáros, as for most Marxists, the issue is not reducible to that of multitude versus working class; it is rather a matter of the organization of social relations and of social wealth and resources.

The totality of capital affects all varieties of labour on a global scale. In an article on global proletarianization, Karl Heinz Roth argues that the proletarianization process occurs primarily through the expropriation of land and the decline of public sector protections for farmers worldwide.[14] The U.S.-led invasion of Iraq, for instance, left more than one million dead and also caused three million peasants to migrate to cities. Peasant migrations are also noticeable in China, the world's second largest economy. In China, after the passing of neoliberal economic reforms, land expropriation transformed small farms into large-scale farming. Civil wars and mass migrations caused similar processes of increased urbanization in Malaysia, Sri Lanka, Tunisia and Morocco. In Latin America, the Caribbean and Southeast Asia, according to Roth, women workers who are easier to control are typically used to replace male workers. This would also be the case in Arab countries had religious practices and oil revenues not kept women away from factory work. Foreign Direct Investment participates in creating uneven development between developing and developed economies.[15] Regardless, declining wages and unemployment are serious problems both in slum cities and in service economies. To make matters worse, the working classes are increasingly drawn away from consciousness of the causes of their poverty toward religious zealotry, ethnic strife and mafia patronage. The consequence of this is the tendency to project fears onto those who represent the interests of the working classes, to demonize socialists and labour parties. The paradox of the anti-globalization movement, especially as it has taken shape in Western countries, is that class consciousness is often a proscribed topic, consigned to the dustbin of history along with Marx and the dialectic. My sense, however, is that those concepts that have emerged from out of the Italian autonomous movement – multitude, precarity, exodus, general intellect, immaterial labour, the primacy of resistance – will increasingly be made to account for their limits and contradictions. In the short term, the fact of proletarianization might not make revolutionary party initiatives any more appealing than they were in the 1950s and 70s, but it gives us pause when we consider that in today's post-political universe revolutionary theory and politics have become almost unimaginable.

The Communist Turn

One of the most insightful critics of the alter-globalization movement is the cultural theorist Slavoj Žižek. In a 2002 interview Žižek plainly stated his skepticism about the anarchist tendency within today's left radicalism.[16] While he agrees with anarchism's goals, Žižek's main concern is that anarchism does nor propose an adequate model of organization. Anarchism, he argues, tends towards both secrecy and authoritarianism. Some kind of authority, usually unaccountable, gets used to safeguard the principle of non-hierarchy. Here Žižek echoes Lacan, who said of the May '68 student protesters that "they're looking for a master, and they will find one." In keeping with Lacanian ethics, Žižek seems to suggest that the anti-capitalist movement does not need to avoid power, but to "produce the master." This is not in order to impose authority, but so that it becomes possible to move towards the "discourse of the analyst." The working-class party, in this case, acts as a mediation of the needs and wishes of the grassroots. "I think if anything," Žižek says, "we need more organization. I think that the left should disrupt this equation that more global organization means more totalitarian control." Further in the interview, Žižek addresses his interest in Lenin. He says:

> I am careful to speak about not repeating Lenin. I am not an idiot. It wouldn't mean anything to return to the Leninist working-class party today. What interests me about Lenin is precisely that after World War I broke out in 1914, he found himself in a total deadlock. Everything went wrong. All of the social democratic parties outside Russia supported the war, and there was a mass outbreak of patriotism. After this, Lenin had to reinvent a radical, revolutionary politics in this situation of total breakdown. This is the Lenin I like. Lenin is usually presented as a great follower of Marx, but it is impressive how often you read in Lenin the ironic line that

"about this there isn't anything in Marx." It's this purely negative parallel. Just as Lenin was forced to reformulate the entire socialist project, we are in a similar situation. What Lenin did, we should do today, at an even more radical level. For example, at the most elemental level, Marx's concept of exploitation presupposes a certain labour theory of value. If you take this away from Marx, the whole edifice of his model disintegrates. What do we do with this today, given the importance of intellectual labour? Both standard solutions are too easy – to claim that there is still real physical production going on in the Third World, or that today's programmers are a new proletariat? Like Lenin, we're deadlocked. What I like in Lenin is precisely what scares people about him – the ruthless will to discard all prejudices.[17]

Though it may seem paradoxical to some, one of the prejudices that Žižek's work has sought to complicate is that of liberal multicultural tolerance. Multiculturalism tends to work against the idea of universalism, which it associates with Eurocentrism. The critique of universalism, however, tends to affirm identities and particularist viewpoints, which, through agonism and hegemonic struggle, it wishes to lend universal validity – a piece of the universalist pie, or a seat at the table. This, however, tends to affirm only a formal or abstract universality, in which all could participate equally. The concrete universal, however, in which we all effectively partake, in one way or another, is that of capitalist exchange. Capital acts as the concrete universal that mediates the various social differences that can be qualified by ethnic particularity, religious difference, gender specificity or even so-called queer indeterminacy. Žižek argues that this postmodern critique of universalism has reached its obvious limitations. As he puts it elsewhere:

in the postmodern 'anti-essentialist' discourse regarding the multitude of struggles, 'socialist' anti-capitalist struggle is posited as just one in a series of struggles ('class, sex and gender, ethnic identity'), and what is happening today is not merely that the anti-capitalist struggle is getting stronger, but that it is once again assuming the central structuring role. The old narrative of postmodern politics was: from class essentialism to the multitude of struggles for identity; today, the trend is finally reversed.[18]

One of the problems with postmodern, post-political social movements, according to Žižek, is that they are not only tolerated by capitalism but encouraged, on the one hand, because they do not pose a serious threat to the system of accumulation, and on the other, because they can sometimes provide an effective measure to be used against socialist politics. Whereas pluralism is allowed, socialism is proscribed. Insofar as the politics of identity cannot be universalized, they prevent radical politicization. What one gets instead is the culturalization of politics, which introduces the modes, codes, markers and styles of victim politics into macro-politics. Only Marxism, according to Žižek, appeals to everyone to adopt the view of the proletariat as a universal class and thereby excludes no one. Postcolonial theory, queer theory, and cultural studies are, according to him, compulsive rituals that talk about change but that oblige nothing determinate to happen at the level of anti-capitalist struggle.

These reflections on post-politics have brought Žižek to ask many times over whether in our political struggles we are anti-capitalist or whether we consider that liberal capitalism with a multicultural face is the least worst of social systems. In this Žižek has the support of the philosopher Alain Badiou, who, in his book *Ethics*, criticizes the ethics of difference, which, Badiou argues, is defeated in advance by its fanaticism and identitarian fixity. Such micro-political strategies, Badiou argues, tend to impose models of behaviour and the promotion of a vulgar sociology, a tourist's fascination with diversity that is indifferent to truth.[19] Fanatics are those who are unable to accept that there can be a truth – human rights for example – that would be the same for everyone. The emphasis on contingency in today's social constructionism takes dialectics out of our understanding of universality, reducing the particular to an element of formal logic, a gesture that is entirely commensurate with the existing world of inequality. In a struggle between class and gender politics, for example, there are two contradictions that can be seen to be effective in any given situation. There is a universal contradiction, the fact that both struggles are determined by conditions established by capitalist relations of production, and a particular contradiction, the fact that the relations of production are conditioned by social relations. In a particular, concrete situation, the capitalist relations of production, the universal dimension, resides literally in the particular contradiction, in the opposition between class struggle and gender struggle.[20] The key point for a materialist critique is that in order for the capitalist relations of production to develop, they may require changes to develop in the social relations of production themselves. Gender struggle might, as a feature of the economic base, further the interests of capital, or, as a feature of the superstructure, appear as a "subjective factor," furthering the interests of people, over and against the concrete, political struggle. We are not surprised to find that the multiple forms of social struggle are prominent on the left, whether in anarchist groups or in social democratic labour unions. The problem here is that this has somehow caused people to believe that subjective interests and social relations are threatened by communist thinking, leading to the view that left liberalism, or pragmatic postmodernism is the political solution to social problems. According to Badiou, the problem then is that we have come to believe that the struggle against capitalism should take a democratic form that would respect the diversity of experiences.[21]

However, if there is an economy of gender, just as there is a economy based on exchange and speculation, our intervention into it should be *political*, as Žižek says, and not *economic*. In the following I wish to make some similar remarks with regard to the economy of culture, which Pierre Bourdieu has shown to be directly related to a social economy of power.[22]

Contemporary Art and Its Discontents

In 2010 the New York City-based public art foundation Creative Time hosted the second Creative Time Summit, titled "Revolutions in Public Practice." The 2010 Summit was the second in a series of conferences that included more than fifty presenters – artists, art collectives, educators, critics and art historians – and was organized into six main clusters on the themes of Markets, Food, Schools, Governments, Institutions, and Plausible Art Worlds.[23] As the title indicates, the conference was not only concerned with definitions of contemporaneity in art, but with the social and political aspects of today's activist forms of art practice. The 2010 Creative Time Summit gives a good indication, I would say, of the manner in which art has begun to respond to the crisis of neoliberal capitalism and has created alternative models of art practice that renew with the belief in the social and political potential of art.

The overall structure of today's social practices, in contrast to traditional studio practices, involves collectivism and reaches out into broad social networks rather than toward gallery and museum audiences. In this sense, they are a continuation of post-60s practices of participatory art and of critical public art and community art practices that developed in the 1980s and 90s. What became apparent in the responses of conference audience members, however, is that many of the artists' projects were based on somewhat naive political foundations, leading to the impression that engaged art has in fact become the "state of the art," the "thing to do" for progressive actors, but without the requisite theoretical analysis. This sometimes results, as Chto Delat member Dmitry Vilensky pointed out, in an almost inarticulate, voluntarist, anarchist tendency based on anti-capitalist moralism and pragmatism. While we may applaud community activism, progressive art practices are often also smiled upon by philanthropic foundations that look for ways to wash their surplus capital. As neoliberal governments gradually withdraw from welfare state provisions, art foundations, development agencies, and even corporations, are increasingly interested in the uses of art as an inexpensive way to manage the social tensions that are a direct outcome of capitalist transformations. On a more mundane level, engaged political art becomes a new way for networked artists to mark their distinction from traditional studio practices.

The ultimate question raised by the Summit, as Vilensky suggested, is whether or not today's engaged artists believe in an alternative to liberal capitalist, parliamentary democracy. The conflicting political viewpoints were somewhat apparent in the structures and themes of the various artworks: free art schools, time-based micro-economies, community-based farming and participatory residencies, ecofriendly farming, market environments within museums, experimental models of economic production based on creative commons licensing, self-instituted artist funding programs, self-instituted and community-based micro-grants programs, critical data mapping projects, ecological and social justice projects, art wage advocacy, rhizomatic recycling projects, and self-instituted exhibition spaces.

The general orientation of these works is an "art in the expanded field" that is informed by the politicized materialist art practices that have been developing since at least the pluralist sixties. One question we might ask of them is the extent to which they are concerned with socialism as opposed to democratic contestation. For many art practitioners, the difference between art and politics has been made largely irrelevant by the development of cultural studies, communications studies, discourse theory, and notions of culture as signifying practice. These methods by and large dispense with old left macro-politics and with ideology critique. In light of this, activist art acts as a new mythic form that attempts to resolve conflicts and contradictions within both the fields of art and politics. However, activist art attempts this as it ceases to consider how culture operates within a neoliberal social framework. In other words, where art ignores the class distinctions on which its own form of effectivity relies, it potentially constitutes a newly mythified form of social practice.

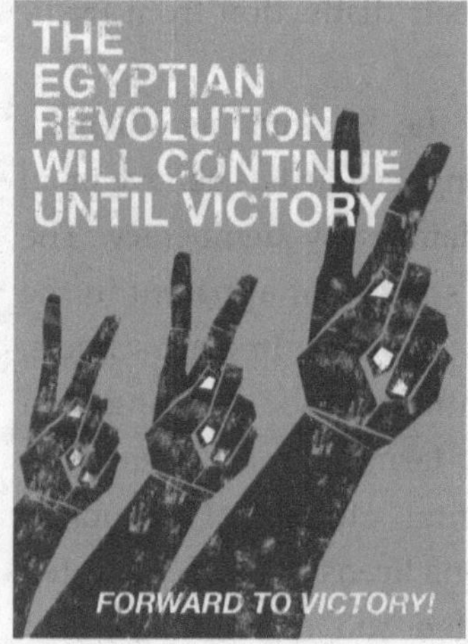

The Egyptian Revolution Will Continue Until Victory – Forward to Victory, 2011. Poster. Source: Internet.

If we are to hold on to the possibility of the social effectivity of art practice today, we should consider two essential problems: the problem of totality and the problem of teleology. When we examine the forms of cultural expression that are most immediately connected to socialist and communist political organization, we typically encounter work that is not concerned with transformations that are specific to the field of cultural production, which is considered to be elitist and serving the self-legitimizing interests of the class of people who manage cultural institutions. A recent example of socialist art, if we agree to call it that, is a poster that circulated on the Internet in February of 2011, in the days before the ouster of the former Egyptian President Hosni Mubarak. It depicts three arms making the peace sign and the words "The Egyptian Revolution Will

Continue Until Victory – Forward to Victory." The colours of the poster are the typical colours of Soviet revolutionary imagery: black, white and red. Revolutionary art like this has no need for institutional legitimation. It is ephemeral and made anonymously to serve a cause. It corresponds to a social need and as such strays from the purposelessness and disinterestedness associated with bourgeois formal culture. One of the problems of this model of activist art for critical practice is that it almost completely leaves the space of institutionalized culture in the hands of neoliberal technocrats who have no difficulty finding artists who can easily insert their productions within the trajectory of formally sanctioned postmodern art practices. Regardless, as the social totality has undergone dramatic transformation and as leftist politics have regained credibility with cultural producers and audiences, institutions have begun to make room for art produced by politicized actors.

The second problem, that of teleology, is by far one of the most interesting problems for art practice. Alfred H. Barr's famous *Timeline of Modern Art* of 1936 is the kind of model of historical development that critics and theorists like to dismiss as irrelevant. They can do so by showing the connections between modernist art and the workings of the capitalist art market. Related to this formalist modernist idea of avant-gardism, Marxist dialectics is sometimes blamed by postmodernists for not only assuming historical progress, as bourgeois philosophy had done, but for pretending to know the direction that progress will take in the future. This of course misses the point of the theory of the communist transition, especially as it was lived in the context of the Russian Revolution, but that fact has not prevented contemporary theorists from looking for alternative models of temporality and becoming. With regard to art practice, perhaps the most incisive use of teleology was that put forward by Peter Bürger in his *Theory of the Avant-Garde*.[24] Bürger's theory of modernism in art distinguishes between the bohemian, historical and neo avant gardes. The first of these includes Realism, Impressionism, Post-Impressionism and Fauvism. Clement Greenberg, in his well-known theory of "avant garde and kitsch," favoured such a "bohemian" view, which understands art mostly in terms of the development of an autonomous sphere of cultural production. Each transgression of the field, by undermining its core principles, and by incorporating contents that are found outside of the normative set of references, works to renew the field. Through the conversion of the products of the bohemian avant gardes into the raw materials of an innovative capitalist cultural framework, Bürger argues, autonomous art tended systematically towards institutionalization. The "historical" avant gardes – Cubism, Futurism, Dada, Constructivism, Surrealism, and Situationationism – sought to challenge this institutionalization of art by making work that reveals the workings of the art system as a feature of class society. One of the means by which the historical avant gardes did this was by radically interweaving their practice with the needs of political movements. The Party artist, for instance, whether described by Vladimir Lenin, Leon Trotsky or Walter Benjamin, worked with an awareness of the limits of art's redemptive promise in a capitalist universe. The "neo" avant gardes, which emerged after the Second World War and in the context of consumer society, are said by Bürger to signal an abandonment of class politics. Given the way that the capitalist culture industries rather than radical politics have (falsely) integrated art into life, art practices associated with New Realism, Fluxus, Minimalism, Conceptualism, Performance, Site Specificity and Institutional Critique, have by and large moved away from practices associated with autonomy and dialectical realism and have instead used the art frame to explore extra-disciplinary forms of knowledge: systems theory, sociology, structuralism, psychoanalysis, feminism, race theory, natural science and ecology, public history and counter-memory.

Post-neo-avant-garde art forms of art, which could not have figured in Bürger's account, could be said in some ways to be post-postmodern, moving away from the concern with culture and representation, and focusing instead on class politics and other kinds of radical practice. In contrast to the historical avant gardes, contemporary practices have developed in the absence of mass social movements like those that once supported social democratic and communist parties. In contrast to the postwar neo-avant gardes, today's art movements are not so much "beyond Moscow and Washington," "beyond left and right," but rather more simply beyond Washington and against the right.

One example from the Creative Time summit could serve to represent the communist tendency that I see emerging among socially engaged art practices. *Guarana Power* is a project organized by the collective Superflex and was first presented at the Venice Biennale in 2003. *Guarana Power* is a softdrink produced with guarana beans that were cultivated by a farmer's co-operative in Maués, in the Brazilian Amazon. Superflex helped farmers to organize against multinational cartels like Nestlé that have driven down the price of guarana beans by eighty percent at the same time that they have been charging higher prices for guarana products. Companies like Nestlé are destroying local communities and creating unemployment. While the farmers have been increasingly underpaid, multinationals have increased their profits. The brand *Guarana Power*, developed by Superflex in collaboration with the Maués farmers, is a glocal brand designed to reclaim the use of guarana as a natural tonic

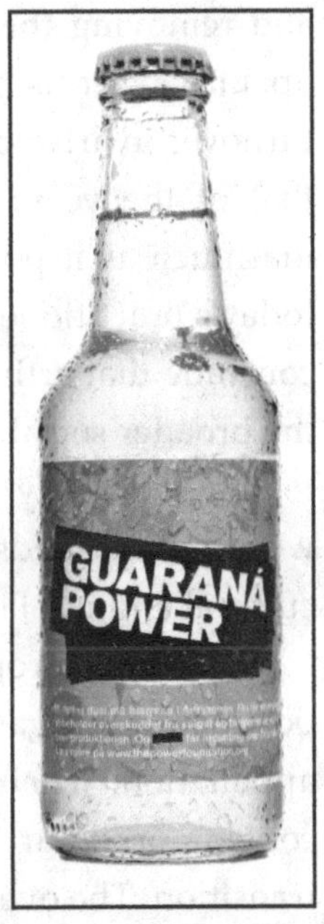

Superflex, *Guarana Power*, 2003. Open source softdrink. Courtesy of Superflex.

and that serves as a forum around which to organize workshops that help people resist the corporate monopoly on raw materials.

It is worth noting that in 1995 the artists Simon Grennan and Christopher Sperandio produced a chocolate bar with the The Bakery, Confectionery and Tobacco Workers' International Union of America Local No. 552. The chocolate bar, called *We Got It!* was made by engaging with union members and nonart audiences in Chicago, taking up the theme of the workers and their trade to allow the workers a greater sense of ownership of their activity. Supeflex's project, made almost ten years later, is slightly different insofar as they are especially interested in questioning and removing the copyright restrictions that allow products to operate in terms of capitalist accumulation. The relatively slow turnover in artworld trends, if we compare this period of time to that of the years 1870 to 1880 or 1910 to 1920, is instructive inasmuch as it points to a stronger tie between the concerns of today's practitioners and the world around them. This leads us to conclude that artists who are working in the expanded sphere of the broader social context are much less concerned with changes to the singularly aesthetic logic of cultural practice, in other words, with trends and the kind of turnover that is demanded by cultural and intellectual markets.

Superflex's project is an example of what we could refer to as post-neo-avant-garde art, though these artists might refuse that appellation. Their work provides a good example of what contemporary art might look like in the context of socialist transition. The overarching difficulty of the new socially engaged practices, as I see it, is that for the most part they dispense with radical political analysis, on the one hand, and aesthetic analysis, on the other. Instead, social relations are associated with the new conditions of (cultural) production – networked sociality, the Internet, affective commons and risk society – bypassing what in older terminology was referred to as the ideological superstructures.[25] In this manner, art reflects rather than challenges the dominant social relations; politics mirrors rather than challenges the predominant relations of production. While this is not always case, what one tends to find today is a reformist biopolitics in which subjects are incited to move away from isolation and individuality towards fairly innocuous forms of collectivity, participation and collaboration. The social function of art within class society is altogether eclipsed by the novelty of the forms of art that proclaim art's irrelevance. The result is that the new practices are often based on the conviction that aesthetic forms and political forms coincide. Art's effectiveness no longer depends on art just as politics is related to a free-floating idea of power and the artist seems concerned with both and neither at the same time. Although they share an ambient radicality, today's post-neo-avant-garde practices do not yet share a common political language that would allow them to organize effectively. The 2010 Creative Time Summit proved to be instructive as it provided important glimpses of the new partisan art forms of our times. Rather than shirk responsibility, the task of today's engaged cultural workers will be to consider how it is that this art can be made more effective and more useful in the struggle against the neoliberal onslaught.

Alterglobal Allegory: Condé and Beveridge Against the Commodification of Water

The final effect is of real figures moving in an unreal, arbitrarily constructed space, the combination of real details in an imaginary framework, the free manipulation of the spatial coefficients purely according to the purpose of the moment.

– Arnold Hauser on "The Concept of Mannerism"

In an essay on the perils and responsibilities of engaged community art activism, the art theorist Declan McGonagle reflects on the work of Toronto-based artists Carole Condé and Karl Beveridge. McGonagle makes two very important assertions about their work. First, he recognizes that Condé and Beveridge "claim no historical allegiance to community art but draw on Conceptual art methodologies that were politicized by Condé and Beveridge, among others, from the mid-1970s on."[1] This is important for McGonagle insofar as community art has been instrumentalized by the art world since roughly the same time, from the 1970s until recently in the guise of relational art.[2] For McGonagle, the limitation of the social significance of art through its reduction to the needs of the art system and the latter's search for the "next big thing" promotes an outmoded modernist model of the avant-garde artist as a tragic figure situated outside the social world. This leads him to his next important point: the rejection of individualism and the re-engagment with the socio-political space through a reflexive and politicized re-engagement with the institutional space. As he puts it:

Condé and Beveridge (...) have worked consistently with an understanding of the distribution zone as the site where value is conferred and have worked to position their practice inside the distribution mechanisms of the "art world," never abandoning that world nor letting it abandon them![3]

The bugbear of McGonagle's essay, however, is universalism. While McGonagle does not want to interpret Condé and Beveridge's work as part of an outdated modernist telos, he does wish to signal the potential role of cultural institutions in fostering progressive social change. Progress can exist on a social level but not on a cultural level. Progress in cultural terms is therefore associated by McGonagle with a culturalization or socialization of politics as opposed to a politicization of culture. The fact that Condé and Beveridge did in fact dedicate themselves very early on to the politicization of culture was recognized by Diana Nemiroff in her review of their exhibition of *Work in Progress* (1981) and *Standing Up* (1981-1982) at the Powerhouse gallery in Montreal. This exhibition, she argued, with its basis in a newly unionized factory and in the history of women workers in general, implied a critique of the art world's illusory view of itself as a collective community.[4]

The postmodern premises of McGonagle's analysis misread the most productive aspects of Condé and Beveridge's work, I would argue, despite the fact that they are there to be read: an understanding of art's imminent unfolding (which of course does not presuppose foreknowledge of historical change but represents the wager of an action that is not grounded in symbolic demands and hegemonic investments) and a thoroughly Hegelian-Marxist understanding that the social relations and modes of production are mediated symbolically, culturally and ideologically. It is in this sense that Condé and Beveridge insist, and as McGonagle is correct to recognize, on institutional determinations as part of the self-alienating yet necessary mediation of art's universal operations. And what is this universal operation if not the workings of capital, the concrete universal against which the universal exception – those among us who are needlessly marginalized, ruined, exploited and killed – takes the form of the class of people in whose name words like emancipation, democracy and justice must, through social struggle, be made meangingful.

Indeed, universality is the principal deadlock of postmodern art criticism, and its avoidance – philosophically, politically and culturally – has done a great deal to prop up a liberal pluralist version of the politics of representation and politics of difference. While we should in no way ignore the forms of struggle that are based on race, gender and sexuality, or those politics that are informed by environmental consciousness and all manner of socially-minded progressive change, it strikes me as odd that much of the recent writing about two of the most leftist of Canadian artists should avoid grappling with leftist political theory. For this I consider an early essay/interview by Martha Fleming to be rather discerning in its numerous references to class analysis. In one matter-of-fact statement, Karl Beveridge sums up much of what goes unrecognized by contemporary artists and theorists:

That argument continues in terms of *proletarianization* of professionals. As the various professions become industrialized, the control over not just the means of production but also the production of meaning begins to fall more and more outside the traditional definition of petit bourgeois control. Professionals and artists become labourers of a kind; other people determine the forms and content of that production of meaning.[5]

Condé and Beveridge's decision in the late 1970s to not merely represent working people but to engage members of labour unions in a collaborative process of meaning production and political representation is directly informed by class analysis and the Marxist labour theory of value. It is this site of struggle that best accounts for the content and real-world references of their work: the life of a working-class family, the lives of working women, the history of Local 222 of the Canadian Auto Workers, the public service in Canada, nuclear power workers, fisheries workers, health and hospital workers, migrant farmworkers, and then some. That Condé and Beveridge have advanced class politics through a process of surfacing "the ideology through the image itself," as Fleming argues, and through the techniques of montage, photo-collage, the multiframe strategies of cartoons and photo-romans, film stills, and advertising, and now, digital compositing – not to mention posters and banners – should, I would argue, be read not in terms of the "politicizing impulse of postmodernism," but in terms of a class politics that is and has been sophisticated enough to fully appreciate the representative alienation that takes the shape of capital, and this, against the direct expressive embodiment of struggle in the form of engaged art practice.[6] For the latter, leading exemplars of the art world's concession to a utopian version of the Fukuyaman "end of history," of the numerous benefits of the "democratic invention" with its endless plurality of public and counter-public spheres, recent historical events – and at the time of this first writing, May 2010, after the killing of dozens of *red shirts* in the capital city of Bangkok and ongoing repression of the Maoist rebels in the Indian hills of Orissa, and later, in October of 2012, after the massacre of more than 40 striking South African mineworkers – have judged that "It's Still Privileged Art."

For critical class-conscious analysis of art and activism, there are positions and pathways beyond the valley of postmodernism, and we could do worse than cite Condé and Beveridge themselves:

The real context within which we work as artists is that of an industrialized culture. The oppositions of fine art and mass media, modernism and realism etc. no longer apply. Culture is divided between dominant and oppositional modes (which in some cases parallel the traditional oppositions) in which oppositional practice must account for both the content and the forms of mass production.[7]

Oppositionality here relates clearly to a social antagonism and the name that history has given to this opposition to the dominant forms of mass culture is *avant-garde*, a term that is philosophically and practically linked with the notions of critical autonomy and political engagement. It is in this frame of reference that it has been possible in recent decades to talk about community *art*, relational *art*, dialogical *aesthetics*, and connective *aesthetics*, for example. For each of these, however, a further positing of the presupposition requires that the new forms of cultural production be brought into critical relation with the political contextualization of cultural production.

A readily acceptable articulation of critical autonomy as social praxis can be noticed in Wolfgang Zinggl's description of contemporary activist art's social purpose:

Art should no longer be venerated in specially designated spaces. Art should not form a parallel quasi-world. Art should not act as if it could exist of itself and for itself. Art should deal with reality, grapple with political circumstances, and work out proposals for improving human coexistence.[8]

However, does this reification of "the social" not abandon the institutionalized sites of mediation that could potentially help to disarticulate the hegemonic links between social relations of production and mode of production? Condé and Beveridge seem to think so when they argue: "if you leave the space [of museums and galleries] empty someone else will fill it, probably with something less critical."[9] They also note that many of these spaces are public institutions and, like other aspects of the collective commons, are worth defending.

While the museum and gallery nexus may very well be the repository of formerly bourgeois and now petty bourgeois technocratic marketing and management, the anarchist exodus from such institutions may not be the best and certainly not the only way to counter the neoliberal ideology of globalized insecurity. Andrea Fraser, a cultural theorist and a practitioner of feminist influenced performance and institutional critique, argues that artists need to grapple not only with changes taking place in society but also within art institutions, which have become almost completely corporatized.[10] Because of this, artists today have taken up some of the theoretical and practical orientations of political activists and have to some degree abandoned the notion that to provide an adequate critique of domination, one must remain forever engaged with the subtleties of textual deconstruction, fearful of a supplemental other that, like the return of the repressed, shadows all totalizing gestures in the name of that which has yet to be. Today's activist artist is indeed more a manipulator of signs than a maker of objects, but meaning in this case is less performative than, as Slavoj Žižek puts it, retroactive: the artist is a self-positing agent whose conscious will to social transformation is not covered by the big Other and no absolute synthesis of the social dialectic is possible. Consequently, many artists today have proposed a renewal with the language of avant-garde and revolutionary action. An example of this can be noticed in the work of the Russian collective Chto Delat, who propose the following:

Contemporary art that is produced as a commodity form or a form of entertainment is not art. It is the conveyor-belt manufacture of counterfeits and narcotics for the enjoyment of a "creative class" sated with novelty. One of our most vital tasks today is unmasking the current system of ideological control and manipulation of people. (...) Because art is an activity open to everyone, neither power nor capital can have a monopoly on the "ownership" of art. One answer to the perennial debate on art's autonomy is the possibility that it can be produced independently of art institutions, whether state or private. In the contemporary conjuncture, the self-negation essential to art's development happens outside institutional practices. As a public form of the unfolding of each person's creative potential, the place of art during moments of revolutionary struggle has always been and will always be in the thick of events, on the squares and in the communes. At such moments, art takes the form of street theater, posters, actions, graffiti, grassroots cinema, poetry, and music. Renewing these forms at this stage in history is the task of the genuine artist.[11]

While Chto Delat is fairly non-dogmatic in their approach to a "common front" of anti-capitalist opposition, it should be said that anarchist politics tend to predominate in the activist world of collectives and alter-global anti-capitalism. Influenced by autonomist post-Marxism (also identified as post-operaism or workerism) and the work of the French theorists Gilles Deleuze and Félix Guattari, critic Brian Holmes argues that we have reached a third phase of institutional critique that moves towards what Gerald Raunig calls "transversal activism," a cultural practice that is made possible by new communications technologies and new social spaces where subjectivity and affect merge with the new forms of cognitive, creative and immaterial labour. As Holmes puts it,

The notion of transversality, developed by the practitioners of institutional analysis, helps to theorize the assemblages that link actors and resources from the art circuit to projects and experiments that don't exhaust themselves inside it, but rather, extend elsewhere. These projects can no longer be unambiguously defined as art. They are based instead on a circulation between disciplines, often involving the real critical reserve of marginal or counter-cultural positions – social movements, political associations, squats, autonomous universities – which can't be reduced to an all-embracing institution. The projects tend to be collective, even if they also tend to flee the difficulties that collectivity involves, by operating as networks. Their inventors, who came of age in the universe of cognitive capitalism, are drawn toward complex social functions, which they seize upon in all their technical detail and in full awareness that the second nature of the world is now shaped by technology and organizational form.[12]

For interventionist artists working in the mode of tactical media, the artist figures as part of the movement of what Marx referred to as the capitalist organization of cooperative labour and the social production of a "general intellect," a shared commons of skills and creativity that produces the conditions for the potential overcoming of individualization and alienation. But as Holmes' work – and that of many other writers influenced by anarchist theory – tends to move away from anything having to do with representation, with social democratic labour unions and political parties especially, it also tends to underestimate or downplay ideology critique in favour of a direct socialization of the modes of production, a subjectivation that takes place almost miraculously without the alienating mediation of what Freud referred to as castration and what Marx described as the fetishism of the commodity. Yet Holmes does not necessarily understand extradisciplinary investigations in the same way that someone like Raunig understands transversal activism. He defines the investigations of groups like Critical Art Ensemble, for example, as an artistic critique of the many disciplines of technology and management that works directly on the sites where ideology is articulated and justified as scientific "truth." There is therefore no consistent or universally agreed upon anarchist line. To take a different example, Paolo Virno argues that there is nothing about the current conditions of neoliberal governmentality and capitalist globalization that dictates the forms that art can and should take. He writes:

To me, engaged art is an integral part of political movements, one of its components. Political movements use a lot of tools, including means of communication like the Internet, and politically engaged art is one of those tools. It is a component of movements' political capital. Yet I would once again like to underline that the most important effect of art is set in the formal sphere. In that sense, even art that is remote from political engagement touches upon the social and political reality. The two are not conflicting matters. They operate on different levels. The formal investigation produces criteria, units of measure, whereas the directly political engagement of the artist is a specific form of political mobilization. (...) Even artists who are remote from the political movement may, through their search for new forms and expressions and in spite of themselves, get in touch with the needs of such a political movement, and may be used by it. Brecht as well as poets much more remote from social realities, like Montale, realized a similar relation. The Situationists were very important when they became a political movement, but from that moment on they were no longer avant-garde art: it's about two modes of existence. They clearly illustrate this double take. Before 1960 they were an artistic movement rooted in Dadaism and Surrealism, afterwards they participated in social resistance, making the same mistakes or gaining the same merits as other political activists. Another problem is that when language becomes the main principle according to which social reality is organized, social reality as a whole becomes aesthetic.[13]

It is this gap that separates art and politics that allows the two to interact and transform each other's economies and it has of course been the error, historically speaking, of revolutionary Marxists to constrain the exploration of aesthetic forms, and for post-operaists in the present to propose a premature synthesis in the name of machinic pragmatism.

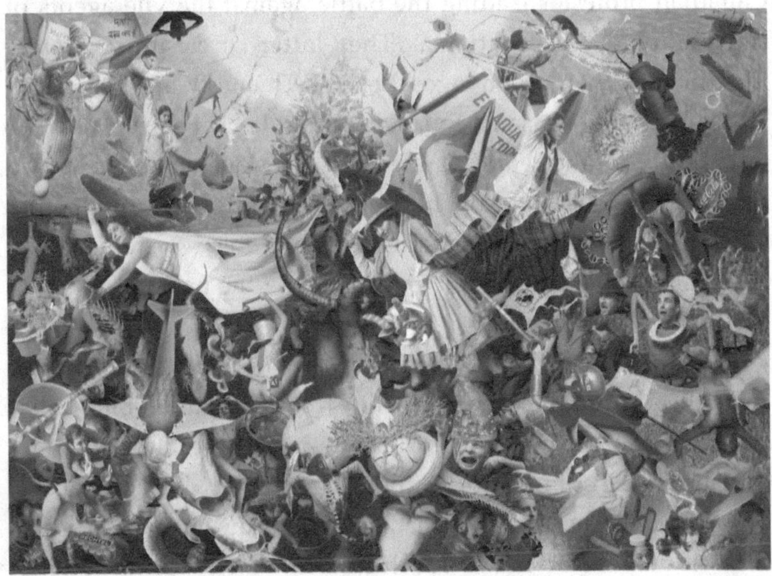

Carole Condé and Karl Beveridge, *The Fall of Water*, 2006-2007. Lightjet, 121.9 x 168.8 cm. Courtesy of the artists.

With this review of some current orientations for politicized art practice, I would like to highlight one of Condé and Beveridge's more recent projects, *The Fall of Water* (2006-2007), a large, digitally-produced allegory of the global struggle against the commodification of water.[14] The work was painstakingly constructed over a period of one year with the artists photographing each figure in separate sittings and compositing the whole piece by piece. The overall effect reproduces the colours and composition of its historical referent, Pieter Bruegel's 1562 painting *The Fall of the Rebel Angels*, in which St. Michael and a host of angels are depicted crushing Lucifer's legion of Bosch-like creatures. The feeling of Breugel's piece, in contrast to what Walter Benjamin says of Baroque allegory, is one of moral assuredness.[15] In fact, Condé and Beveridge could be said to have rendered this Counter-Reformation work somewhat comical, with a Bolivian indigenous woman, a South Asian activist and a Canadian protester leading the battle against the vile agents of transnational corporations. The latter are appropriately identified by their brand logos: Bechtel, Thames Water, American Water, Vivendi, Dasani, Evian, Coca Cola, Pepsi, Nestlé. The tattered flag of the World Bank is tied to a skeleton key held by a figure wearing a riot cop helmet. The World Bank and other similar institutions of global finance are in this way represented as holding some sort of key to unravelling the balance of power between good and evil.

Dot Tuer has made the argument that *The Fall of Water* represents the philosophico-political shift from proletarian blue-collar struggle to the post-revolutionary multitude described by thinkers like Paolo Virno, Antonio Negri and Michael Hardt.[16] This in some ways does support the humourous manner in which the evil demons do not so much look like the personification of malevolence but more like petty bourgeois yuppies (maybe even the proverbial kind who read Deleuze), mere functionaries of global knowledge industries. It's as though, as Hardt and Negri argue in *Empire*, the advanced stage of digital capitalism requires little more than a slight shift of perspective for the self-valorization of labour to be actualized in our times. According to Condé and Beveridge, the post-revolutionary idea of the multitude might in some ways be somewhat utopian and its proponents not always clear about just how it is that the transition to global democracy can actually take place.[17] What can be stated, nevertheless, is that workers' struggles have effectively joined up with indigenous struggles, with those of the Palestinians, for instance, and those who oppose mega projects like the damming of the Narmada River. As the various World Social Forums and alter-globalization protests have created new possibilities for workers to join their struggles and analyses and offer new alternatives to the neoliberal ideology of free markets, the global falling rates of profit and the environmental catastrophes that are being caused by overproduction and global warming keep the now interconnected international economies and trading blocks in a tight embrace. Distant peoples that in the sixteenth century were only known to Europeans as allegorical figures are now not only nameless maquiladora workers but also familiar leaders, activists, writers and journalists engaged in the global struggle against neoliberal capitalism.

If the leaders of the 2010 World People's Conference on Climate Change have called for the recognition of the Universal Declaration on the Rights of Mother Earth, then certainly there is a cultural expression that can contribute, in its own way, by heralding a proposed change in governance. Ten years before the recent Conference in Cochabamba, Bolivian protesters and social justice activists successfully prevented the privatization of the city's water supply by the multinational giant Bechtel. This event is only one of many cases in which neoliberal economic policies have met with organized resistance and without a doubt there is increasing awareness of how state governments everywhere have mortgaged the very survival of humanity to rotten speculators. It is fitting then that *The Fall of Water* was sold to a Bolivian neurosurgeon while on view as part of the touring exhibition organized by the Agnes Etherington Art Centre. This patron has donated the work to the National School of Art in La Paz, Bolivia, where it will serve as an example of contemporary art that is based in the forms of Counter-Reformation art that have become part of the popular artistic traditions of that country.

By Any Means Necessary: From the Revolutionary Art of Emory Douglas to the Art Activism of Jackie Sumell

In a well-known debate with the cultural and political theorists Judith Butler and Ernesto Laclau, Slavoj Žižek put forward one of his most prescient criticisms of the postmodern cultural politics of difference, that is, the view that because capital functions as the concrete universal of our global situation, the categories of race, class, gender and sexuality do not operate as equivalent categories of difference and oppression.[1] Žižek asks us to consider how it is that class analysis allows us to distinguish a universal emancipatory radical politics from the plurality of struggles that are based on race, gender and sexuality, which today functions as the basis of a neoliberal "post-politics" that leads to what he refers to as the "culturalization of politics."[2] He argues that in the chain of signifiers race, class and gender, class is named but rarely theorized. In his book on Iraq, he makes the following claim: "The first step is already accomplished: from the multitude of struggles for recognition to anti-capitalism; what lies ahead is the next, 'Leninist', step – towards politically organized anti-capitalism."[3] While many in the art world are prepared to concede that neoliberal capitalist politics are fundamentally anti-democratic, few are prepared to take this "next step" and "make capitalism history." Even Alain Badiou, who argues that the "communist hypothesis" must be upheld against today's reactionary restoration of class power, believes that the Leninist sequence of a vanguard party organization and a mass mobilization of the proletariat is one that is no longer an option.[4]

In relation to this discussion, I wish to consider the exemplary leadership of the Black Panther Party, which was particularly active in the years 1966 (one year after the assassination of Malcolm X) to 1982 (although it is still active today), and which was the target of the most intense domestic counter-intelligence effort in American history. I discuss this specifically in relation to the cultural production of revolutionary art in the service of the people and the Panthers' Ten-Point Program for Self-Determination, which demanded full employment, an end to the oppression of black communities, decent housing, radical education, health care, an end to police brutality, an end to wars of aggression, and the end of the racist prison system.[5] I do this with an eye to situating revolutionary art in the context of today's socially engaged art activism and in particular, with reference to Jackie Sumell's collaboration with Herman Wallace in the *The House That Herman Built* (2003, ongoing).

The Panthers and the Politics of Class Struggle

Mike Kelley once asserted that "It will be a cold day in hell when you see a major museum mount a show of the cultural production of the Weather Underground or Black Panthers."[6] That day turned out to be not too far off and its focus in the visual arts has been the work of the Panthers' Minister of Culture, Emory Douglas, and the revolutionary art that he produced for the *Black Panther Newspaper*, which was published between the years 1967 and 1979 and which, at its peak in 1970, had a circulation of over 400,000. Douglas' reflections on his role as Minister of Culture were published in an article titled "Revolutionary Art/Black Liberation," which appeared in *The Black Panther* in the May 18, 1968 issue. The function of revolutionary art, he states, is to illuminate the party, which educates the masses of black people, via pictures. Those who read the *BP* newspaper are not readers, he asserts, but activists. Douglas' work combined socialist realism with social realism and caricature. The radical tone of his words in this piece, which asserts the need to "draw deadly pictures of the enemy," reflects the Panther orientation towards self-defense and its dissatisfaction with the Civil Rights Movement's principle of nonviolence. This same year, however, and with the increasing pressure placed on party leadership as well as infiltration by agents provocateurs, the party shifted its focus on survival programs, as they were called, such as free breakfasts for children and health clinics, as well as running party members in local, state and national electoral races.

In 2004 an exhibition titled "A Retrospective on the Black Panther Party and The Art of Emory Douglas" was held at the Sargent Johnson Gallery at the African American Art and Culture Complex in San Francisco. In 2008, "Black Panther: The Revolutionary Art of Emory Douglas" opened at LA MoCA's Pacific Design Center, and in 2009 "Emory Douglas: Black Panther" was held at New York City's New Museum. The last two exhibitions were curated by artist and cultural historian Sam Durant, who also edited an illustrated catalogue of Douglas' work.[7] Two of the essays in Durant's catalogue allow us to consider the basic opposition between a political struggle that involves cultural production and a culturalized politics. Emblematic of the latter is artist and theorist Colette Gaiter's "What Revolution Looks Like." Although Gaiter has a deep appreciation of Douglas' illustrations of the harsh reality of the life of the disenfranchised, she assumes that the revolutionary ambitions of the Black Panthers have been accomplished, and places black liberation in the context of other minority struggles led by students, women, the disabled, gays, and lesbians. She writes: "That fact that we now take these changes for granted is a paradox. Activists and revolutionaries like the Black Panthers worked to make ideas that were once believed to be extreme – like equal opportunity for all Americans – seem like the natural order of things."[8] Gaiter's use of the past tense and her suggestion that the major struggles of the 1960s were over by 1970 assumes quite a great deal about the current state of world politics, especially as the U.S. is involved in imperialist wars of aggression in Iraq, Afghanistan and Pakistan, and as it condones the right-wing politics of oligarchic and corporate control in Asia, Latin America, Africa, the Middle East *and* at home. Kathleen Cleaver's contribution to the book, which recounts the series of events from 1967 to 1969, somehow seems more actual and pertinent, decrying the American military behemoth and declaring solidarity with all of those involved in revolutionary guerrilla battles and fighting imperialism.

The theme of revolutionary struggle is also taken up in Durant's book by Greg Jung Morozumi, curator of the Sargent Johnson Gallery exhibition and former member of the radical group I Wor Kuen. In his essay, "Emory Douglas and the Third World Cultural Revolution," Morozumi links the Panthers' activities with those of other anti-racist organizations, specifically the Young Lords, the Brown Berets and the Red Guard. Linking Mao's writings on mass organization with Fanon's anti-colonial "handbook of the cultural revolution," *The Wretched of the Earth* (1961), Morozumi emphasizes how the Panthers' struggle became international, with reissues of Emory's art in Cuba, Algeria, Vietnam and China, and with various struggles coming together. For Morozumi, solidarity against Western colonialism, the principle of self-defense and revolutionary violence against oppressors are served by artists who solidify the revolutionary consciousness of the people and, as such, take on a vanguard role against dispossession. "Rather than reinforcing the cultural dead end of 'post-modern' nostalgia," he writes, "the inspiration of [Douglas'] art raises the possibility of rebellion and the creation of new revolutionary culture."[9]

Here I wish to consider one of the obstacles to revolutionary theory in contemporary cultural discourse, namely, the concept of masculinism. A well-rehearsed charge against the Black Panthers is that their politics were masculinist. A common counter-argument is that sexism and patriarchy were found not only in Panther praxis, but in society at large in the 60s and 70s. However, masculinism can also be used as a critique of any politics that asserts itself as a universalizing discourse and thus, ostensibly, presupposes a singular social consciousness. A good example of the charge of Panther masculinism can be found in Erika Doss's essay, "'Revolutionary Art Is a Tool for Liberation': Emory Douglas and Protest Aesthetics at the *Black Panther*," which argues that the Panthers' effort to uphold black masculinity in the face of liberal white racist society was fraught with heterosexist and homophobic manifestations.[10]

According to post-colonial theorist Homi Bhabha, masculinism is not simply about the social authority invested in men, but describes the "sublation of social antagonisms" and the "repression of social division" into an impersonal universal discourse.[11] Feminist psychoanalysis holds that such fantasies of political unity presume a coherent social universe as well as a stable subjective reference point that cannot be sustained, and that therefore produces its notion of social reality through a series of exclusions and occluded possibilities. Former Panther and intellectual activist Angela Davis has asserted that the theory of masculinism was nonexistent in the 1960s and is only now an important concept within radical theory.[12] The point of radical politics, I would argue, is to assert a universal emancipatory project against political pragmatism and with the full acknowlededgement of the ungrounded basis of political choice. Kathleen Cleaver is only one among many Panther leaders to assert that gender issues in the Party were not as important as revolutionary struggle. She writes:

It seemed to me that part of the genesis of the gender question, and this is only an opinion, lies in the way it deflects attention from confronting the revolutionary critique our organization made of the larger society, and turns it inward to look at what type of dynamics and social conflicts characterized the organization. (...) How do you empower an oppressed and impoverished people who are struggling against racism, militarism, terrorism, and sexism too? That's the real question.[13]

Two things can be said about the problems of contemporary post-structural theory as it is commonly practiced. The first relates to cultural theory and the problematic assumptions of social constructionism; the second relates to the way that difference politics leads to a form of ultra-politics that prevents an adequate analysis of the status of the political. While social constructionism makes the necessary assertion of the groundless nature of social processes, it tends to operate in politically correct cultural milieux as a kind of false consciousness thesis, against which liberals assert their distance from meta-political class politics. In his critique of social constructionism, sociologist Michael Schudson argues that postmodern theorizing tends to lead to an impoverished view of political action by collapsing lived social experience with culture.[14] The theoretical emphasis on preconstituted social structures and the discursive situation of "subjects" provides a seemingly sophisticated basis for social criticism. However, in its common usage, it leaves little room for the constitution of knowledge that is independent of ideology and positionality. All knowledge is reduced to the calculus of power. Rather than deny the world – as well as human agency – Schudson argues for an understanding of the relationship between knowledge and the world. For our purposes, the revolutionary art of the Black Panthers would thus require an adequate grounding in an understanding of the "autonomy of culture in human affairs."[15] This is not to argue that culture is neutral or innocent, but it is a necassry gesture if the left wishes to leave no political presuppositions free from critical examination. To reduce culture to power and interestednesss, Schudson explains, trivializes culture and fails to recognize politics. By simply invalidating everything with notions like undecidability, and by seeking to blur boundaries and deconstruct the oppositions they generate, cultural studies scholars tend to invalidate any critical social project.

When postmodernists make political assertions, they typically take a pragmatic route that starts by denouncing any and all claims to universality, behind which lie contingent, particularistic interests that are codified most often as white male patriarchy. The problem with particularistic politics that assert the personal as political, Žižek argues, is that they cannot be universalized. Žižek criticizes identity politics by contesting Jacques Rancière's distinction between the political (social agonism, dissensus) and politics (police functions, the state) and by suggesting that only a politics that can universalize its claims and enforce them with official laws and police functions can claim to be a radical politics. Postmodern post-politics that foreclose a radical universalization of struggle lead ultimately to a politics of liberal multicultural tolerance. They amount to something similar to what Žižek defines as ultra-politics:

> the attempt to depoliticize conflict by way of bringing it to extremes. (...) In ultrapolitics, the repressed political returns in the guise of the attempt to resolve the deadlock of political conflict by its false radicalization – that is, by reformulating it as [not a war of emancipation, but] a war between us and them, our enemy, where there is no common ground of symbolic conflict.[16]

In this, contemporary micro-politics, despite its theoretical conceits, often operates a similar deradicalization of politics that benefits the conservative right.

The exemplar of ultrapolitics is the Nazi legislator Carl Schmitt. In Schmittean political struggle, political agents need not hold to the letter and accountability of the law, but may act in their narrow interests by attacking those that they suspect of enemy status. The Schmittean agent acts according to the obscene underside of the law and its unspoken rules, without taking recourse to the law and its institutional mechanisms. Such post-politics is in fact the basis of what Angela Davis and Bettina Aptheker defined in 1971 as the "infirmities" of the bourgeois democratic state and its repressive judicial system and prisons.[17] According to Davis, the political prisoner is the person who breaks a law for the sake of the collective welfare and survival of a people, and thus violates the unwritten laws that prohibit disobedience to a repressive system. When a political prisoner breaks a law, it is not that particular law that forms the basis of her prosecution, but the unwritten law. According to fascist legal theory, the political prisoner is guilty *a priori*: "Anyone who seeks to overthrow oppressive institutions, whether or not he has engaged in an overt illegal act, is *a priori* a criminal who must be buried away in one of America's dungeons."[18] Needless to say, the history of the repression of the Black Panther Party is one that involves such anti-democratic and counter-revolutionary uses of the judiciary and penal system.

The relative critical autonomy of art allows for a measure of distance from politics. Because of this, art has often been the target of political control. Today's socially engaged artists share no coherent set of principles even if, as socially minded activists, they share similar ideals. Insofar as vanguard art and politics are decried as masculinist universalism, a radical emancipatory agenda for culture cannot be imagined, let alone put into practice. The contemporaneity of Black Pather struggles is therefore perhaps a good place to start for some idea of what can be done to fight the neoliberal assault on working people.

Revolutionary Fame and Tobasco Sauce

Perhaps one of the most egregious cases of unmitigated injustice is the prosecution of the Angola 3: Albert Woodfox, Herman Wallace and Robert King Wilkerson. Although King was released from the Louisiana State Penitentiary in 2001, his comrades continue to serve life sentences in solitary confinement for the alleged 1972 murder of a prison guard. This conviction is largely recognized as wrongful and designed to silence the three Black Panther activists, who have struggled for prison reform, to end prison rape, and to improve the inhumane conditions that prevail in places like the Louisiana State Penitentiary.[19] Formerly an antebellum slave plantation, today the prison complex is a 180,000-acre work camp where three quarters of the inmates are African-American. As the largest employer in the region, the Louisiana State Penitentiary pays prisoners anywhere between four and twenty cents per hour for their forced labour.

I learned about the Angola 3 through a remarkable video project produced by the Brooklyn-born activist artist Jackie Sumell. Sumell was moved by a lecture given by Robert King in California and from there began a correspondence with Herman Wallace, who has been living in a 6 x 9 foot cell for more than forty years, a situation that she refers to as a "psychological mind fuck."[20] Wallace is forced to remain in this cell for twenty-three hours per day, seven days per week. In a 2003 letter, Sumell asked Wallace, "What kind of house does a man who has lived in a 6 x 9 foot box for over thirty years dream of?" Wallace's response became the basis of *The House That Herman Built*, an ongoing collaborative project between Sumell and Wallace.

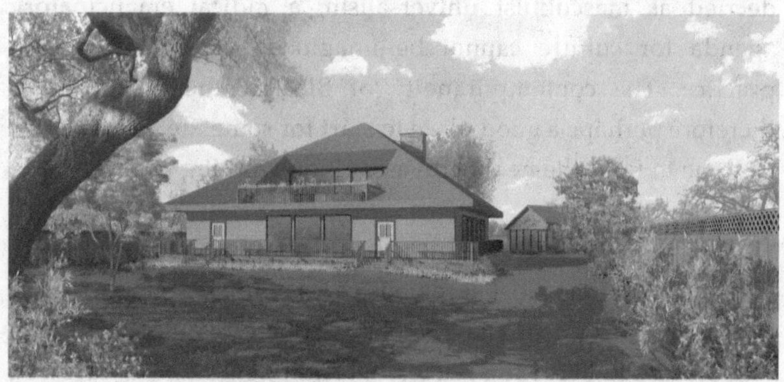

Jackie Sumell, *The House That Herman Built*, 2006. CAD video with sound recording. Stills from video. Courtesy of Jackie Sumell.

As part of this extensive collaboration, Sumell produced a video featuring a CAD architectural drawing based on Wallace's written description of his ideal home, as narrated by King. The video opens with an exterior view of the house, surrounded by gardens and flowers. From a two-car garage, the viewer passes a storage space with a pantry for dry goods. In his review of the project, Wallace noticed that among the items represented in the pantry, Sumell had forgotten the Tobasco sauce. The fact that Wallace noticed such a tiny omission shows the extent to which the project allows him to imagine himself in a wholly different place, freed from confinement.

Among the many splendid aspects of the house, most striking is Wallace's commitment to revolutionary politics, as evidenced in the dining and conference room with its wall of revolutionary fame displaying framed pictures of the prominent abolitionists John Brown, Gabriel Prosser, Harriet Tubman, Nat Turner, and Denmark Vessey. The Black Panther Party emblem is painted at the bottom of the swimming pool in the yard. Wallace's experiences of militant struggle are reflected in the design of the house, which allows for a quick escape. A fireplace in the second-floor master bedroom leads to an underground bunker thirty-five feet away from the house, equipped with military essentials, foodstuffs, and first aid supplies. Wallace's description vacillates between details concerning construction materials, the size of rooms and their furnishings, and uncanny reminders of life in prison and yearnings for a just society. "I wonder," Wallace concludes, "how psychologists would evaluate me as a person."

The House That Herman Built has been exhibited widely in North America and Europe, and with the encouragement and donations of architects, designers, builders, artists, an urbanist and a documentary filmmaker, plans to build *Herman's House* are underway. I interviewed Jackie Sumell in person and by email in February and March of 2010. I inquired about the relationship between the activist organizing of the present and the revolutionary goals and aims of the Black Panther Party.

Marc James Léger: How are Herman Wallace and Albert Woodfox doing? How do you think *Herman's House* has so far contributed to their cause?

Jackie Sumell: I would suggest that you write to Herman and Albert and ask them these questions. They are truly remarkable men who are visibly exhausted by four decades of injustice. They maintain a strong sense of balance because they believe their case will serve to correct the criminal justice system. Relative to the second part of your question, it is an enormous compliment to hear them say that *The House That Herman Built* has been the greatest tool in raising awareness about their case. Obviously that is my greatest motivation.

MJL: You've mentioned somewhere that you situate your work between art and activism. Could you tell me some more about that? How would you situate your work in relation to the art of Emory Douglas?

JS: Well, I am an activist and an artist and a sister and a friend and a godmother and many other things, so it's less the case that my work is situated between art and activism and it's more a case that these various aspects of my life are influences on my work. As far as any comparisons with the work of Emory are concerned, Emory *is* a Black Panther – he didn't study it, he doesn't reflect on it based on the words of others, he lives it. It is totally different. Emory's work was critical to a radical movement and the trajectory of radical thinking in the 1970s. His work could have cost him his life. What I do is very different. Yes, there are great risks involved but the priorities and risks are different when compared to a black man in the 70s who was creating the visual vocabulary for a radical campaign of self-determination.

MJL: In a meeting we had a few weeks ago, I noticed that you took exception to the words "anger" and "militancy" when said in relation to the Black Panthers. Recently I read this statement by Emory Douglas about his frustration with the Civil Rights

Movement in the 60s: "The thing was that I hadn't been able up to that time to apply my anger to my drawing and painting." An essay by Erika Doss that I read goes out of its way to emphasize the masculinism of the Panthers. I'm wondering if your hesitancy about terms like "militancy" are part of a feminist response to this history or if it's part of the way people today look at revolutionary class politics in general. Another way to phrase this question might be to ask you what you think about the relation of revolutionary struggle to activism.

JS: This feels like two diverging questions. I understand Emory's anger completely. I don't think that I took exception to the word anger in relation to the BPP. I think it was in reference to Robert King in particular, who transformed his anger into constructive action and reaction. I am sure that Emory, as a young black man living under the oppressive regimes of the 60s had *beaucoup* of that anger – and rightfully and righteously so. I think that today he might also say that he found a constructive outlet for that anger, and it has been effective. We today can share that experience. I can also reflect on anger as something that is not constructive. I respect anger as an important emotion, equal to love or sadness, but like the latter two it has to be channeled or it can isolate itself and become destructive.

As for misogyny in the Panthers, I never read Erika Doss's work, nor do I know what you are referencing, but I would say that a transformative moment came for me when I realized that the Black Panther Platform was about equality and self-determination for all poor and oppressed people regardless of race, gender, or sexual orientation. Associating the Panthers with misogyny is consistent with the tactics of COINTELPRO [the FBI's Counter-Intelligence Program against the Panthers and other revolutionary groups] and is used to slander the movement. The Black Panther Party was comprised of human-doings and was fueled by people power and a need for change. Sure, mistakes are implicit in redesigning the way an entire society functions. I am not suggesting that the Black Panther Party was a flawless solution or that acts of perceived misogyny or prejudice did not take place. They themselves were learning in the process of acting, whatever their intentions. That was and is progressive thinking, even if things are never as perfect as we would like them to be. I wasn't there but I do have relationships with very strong and visible Panther ladies who would speak in opposition to these kinds of characterizations.

MJL: What can you tell me about Herman Wallace's involvement in the Black Panther Party? Judging by his vision of the House, the theory and practice of the Panthers is still very much alive for him. Of course, in the context of forty years of solitary confinement, this praxis is directly connected to prison reform for himself and for other political prisoners.

JS: I can tell you that Herman Wallace is a Black Panther. It is an ideology and a commitment that is independent of history or the fact that the Party was targeted and subsequently dissolved by the U.S. Government in 1974. The principles of the Black Panther Party survive Herman. His marriage to the Party provides him with a focus that allows him to survive because he realizes that struggle is selfless. It is about change for the greater good and for the people. He understands that he is a representative of some of the greatest miscarriages of justice in this lifetime and that he has to survive in order to ensure that no one else will have to endure what he has. Albert and Robert both uphold these principles. It is where they meet, where they define fraternity. The Black Panther Platform guides them.

After this correspondence with Sumell I wrote to Herman Wallace and asked him a related series of questions. His response letter came to me dated March 24, 2010. It was opened and stamped: "Prison mail. Not censored. Not responsible for contents. Elayn Hunt Correctional Center." It reads:

Warm Greetings, Marc,

At this very moment I am swamped with legal work that demands the utmost of my attention, but, putting something aside that I consider equally important oftentimes becomes my biggest negative distraction. So, I decided to put everything aside and get back with you. Thank you for taking an interest in the work that Jackie and I are doing, as it is through the process of this work that she seems to be defining herself.

On 3-4-10 she took a flight and left for Germany and will be there for two months and I am going to miss our talks and visits.

I find you have a vast resume in the field of art. Art is indeed your specialty – mine is not. It is dangerous for Albert and I to discuss Panther matters at this time. The government is using every piece of evidence they can against us, no matter how small, to win a third conviction against Albert. So, I'm not sure how effective I will be in assisting you in your request.

I'm convinced that your interest rests around how activist art and revolutionary art can be connected – reconnected. In connecting activist art with revolutionary art there must be a recognition of a definite political lineage. We live in a class society and each class has its own culture and the literature that expresses it. Revolutionary culture creates an ideological front prior to the revolution. To effectively bring on an end to what we recognize as the prison-industrial complex, we must make the connection with the present social order. It's not about calling for an end to the facilities of prisons, jails, or penitentiaries – it's about reflecting upon the laws, conditions and many other social orders if we are to effectively transform these facilities. *The House That Herman Built* is to certify that the literature and the art connect with an understanding of the ways of creating institutions, ideas, and strategies – as Angela Davis points out – "strategies that will render prisons obsolete."

How are we doing? Not good, Marc; not good at all. In 2008 federal judge James Brody overturned Albert's conviction and from that point the government has come out with full force, attacking both Albert and I with lies. They attacked Albert for defending himself against the Attorney General's lies, daring to challenge his power, and locked the both of us back up in solitary. I'm presently in a worse place than Closed Cell Restriction [the solitary confinement at Angola where Albert is kept]. I've been here for five months and eleven days.

You asked how do I think *Herman's House* contributed to our cause and the cause of other political prisoners. This house and the ideas and ideals that embrace it could not have been possible had it not been for the artist, Jackie Sumell. The house is actually a people's house. The building of this house has so far brought hundreds of people together. It has brought together artists, activists, designers, rich and poor. It is recognized by students around the world and recently, Occidental College had forty of its students in New Orleans work on rebuilding New Orleans and Angola 3 projects. These students set up a tour of Angola Penitentiary and visited the notorious Camp J and Angola's Death House. This tour was made possible as a result of the artistic criterion born out of the unity of art and politics. This brings me back to a part of your interest when you referred to a "reconnection." There was never a disconnection of activist and revolutionary art. Within the class struggle, you will always find the political criterion first and the artistic criterion following. In building my House, Jackie connects it with 38 years of my being forced to live here in a six-by-eight-foot cell. She recreates the cell – a new cell for every exhibition worldwide. This house project has been instrumental in connecting me with many people internationally. I, in turn, connect them with each other, either personally or through the unification of *The House That Herman Built* website.

On the subject of Panther culture, such derives from the nature of the Black Panther in general. First and foremost, it is a defensive animal who will only attack when threatened. So far as I can only tell you of my own social or caged experience as a Panther, but even at this point it is legally advised of me not to, but I will tell you that we all are guided by the ideology of the Ten-Point Program.

I can relate to Mike Kelley's statement. However, such ideas will not display my form of force primarily because its political viewpoint is incorrect. *The House That Herman Built* is tightly connected with the movement of the Angola 3. Consider the absolute fact of the American government priding itself on being a democratic system – the land of the free – a government that is known to chastise other nations on human rights violations and the holding of political prisoners. As a result, the Angola 3 are political prisoners and have been kept in solitary confinement for the past 38 years. Through the artistic skills of Jackie Sumell and other artistic values such as "Life's Morcel," a play produced by Linda Carmichael; "Angola 3," a play produced by Parnell Herbert; "3 Black Panthers," a documentary narrated by Mumia Abu-Jamal and produced by Jimmy O'Halligan; and on March 26, 2010, "In the Land of the Free," a Roddick Foundation Film narrated by Samuel L. Jackson, we present to the world, art in motion.

All Power to the People

Herman

Among the prohibitions that work against the radicalization of culture and politics is the view that the avant-garde, both in terms of political party organization and in terms of an autonomous cultural resistance to art as an instrument of capitalist exchange, is thought to be part of an exhausted ideology. According to Brian Holmes, the vanguard today is the global process itself, the "second modernity" of today's risk and security regimes.[21] In light of this, he argues, what remains to be done is the construction of institutions that are able to transform the destructive forces that prevail. As part of this reflection, the legacy of the Black Panther Party and the ongoing struggle of the Angola 3 remind us that much of what is called racism in the U.S. and elsewhere is, as Noam Chomsky states, directly related to an unpronounceable five-letter word, namely: *class*.[22] As democratic institutions become evacuated of content, Chomsky says, people look for a political saviour or turn to religious fanaticism.

While it is true that the totality of neoliberal capital creates resistance to it in the form of activism, the passage from the abstract to the concrete universal allows us to understand the radically contingent space that is opened up as art like that produced by Herman Wallace and Jackie Sumell represents class struggle by other means. While today's activist art may seem less revolutionary than the exemplary leadership of the Black Panthers in the 60s and 70s, we should insist on the way that it retroactively reconstructs the global situation in the contingency of necessity, and allows us to consider what an effective form of revolutionary art might look like today.

Afterthoughts on Engaged Art Practice: ATSA and the State of Emergency

> The tradition of the oppressed teaches us that the "state of emergency" in which we live is not the exception but the rule. We must attain a conception of history that is in keeping with this insight. Then we shall clearly realize that it is our task to bring about a real state of emergency, and this will improve our position in the struggle against Fascism.
> – Walter Benjamin

It has been the purpose of twentieth-century avant-garde art, in Clement Greenberg's famous formulation, "to find a path along which it would be possible to keep culture moving in the midst of ideological confusion and violence."[1] Today, much contemporary activist art operates with strategies that have been worked out in Situationist, actionist, site-specific, community, and context art, and that has as its purpose the possibility of keeping progressive politics moving. Contemporary engaged art practices have been described in varying ways by the critics and artists Mary Jane Jacob, Suzanne Lacy, Miwon Kwon, Claire Bishop, Grant Kester, and Bruce Barber.[2] Given the relative insouciance of contemporary activists for artistic consecration, it is fair to say, as Brian Holmes argues, that the radical art of the 2000s has undergone a phase change and that, for the most part, it no longer looks to the field of art production for the validation of meaning and effectivity.[3] This I argue is an adequate starting point for an analysis of the activist work of the Montreal art duo Annie Roy and Pierre Allard, better known as the collective ATSA (Action Terroriste Socialement Acceptable/Socially Acceptable Terrorist Action). ATSA figures among the many activist artist collectives that in the years following the emergence of the alter-globalization movement in the late 1990s have joined the ranks of what, for lack of a unifying term, we could call socially engaged artists.

Since 1998, ATSA has produced multifaceted activist interventions in public places. The 2009 instance of its yearly project on the state of homelessness in Montreal, *État d'Urgence* (State of Emergency), provides an opportunity to consider changes in the field of critical public art that have occurred over the past decade. ATSA's work provides an occasion to reflect on what has been gained inasmuch as critical community art has made its way into and out of mainstream discourse, and also what has been lost, insofar as certain strategies become the stock-in-trade of an administered culture. In this we should recall Martha Rosler's influential 1981 essay "In, Around, and Afterthoughts (On Documentary Photography)," which assails the liberal humanist assumptions of traditional photojournalism.[4] Community art has for some time worked to provide solutions to a faltering welfare state bent on environmental destruction, enormous military expenditures, and an inability to come to terms with the failure of neoliberal economics. For some activists, community action becomes a way to bypass institutions of representative democracy and to directly create non-capitalist forms of association. Such activism is clearly not based on a perception of wrongs that, as Rosler says about liberal documentary journalism, are unrelated to the social system that not only tolerates them but creates them. For Greenberg's idea of ideological confusion, then, we should simply identify the problem of ideology as such, and on this score ATSA's issue-oriented work reveals ideological and political struggles. The strength of a work, Marxists have argued, does not rely on the presentation of a correct ideological position but is mediated by the relative autonomy of the field of cultural production. A critical evaluation of today's engaged art in the context of a phase change thus requires an appreciation of what such a change promises: the re-evaluation of community art inasmuch as it has been guided by liberal pluralist politics.

One of the most succinct expressions of contemporary activist art's social purpose is Wolfgang Zinggl's assertion:

> Art should no longer be venerated in specially designated spaces. Art should not form a parallel quasi-world. Art should not act as if it could exist of itself and for itself. Art should deal with reality, grapple with political circumstances, and work out proposals for improving human coexistence.[5]

Art practices, however, do not emerge from nowhere but rely on the modification of existing models. An engaged art practice is more often than not decidedly leftist and maintains, as Barber argues, the lessons learned from successful avant-garde models from the past.[6] Notwithstanding the "beyond left and right" mantra of postmodern academics, the left is hardly a monolithic bloc, and longstanding disputes continue to animate the movement. We find, consequently, analogous differences within the political left and the artistic left. As Nato Thompson puts it in relation to tactical media,

> There is no political consensus among interventionists. Interventionism is not a political movement disguised as art. Practices and ideologies among interventionists vary greatly... They represent methods of protest and public education integrally connected to larger social movements. And while there are extraordinary differences of opinion regarding how and what social changes should be brought about, it is also true that many artists seem to agree that the current political climate is dangerous.[7]

We could argue, then, that the minimum political programme of engaged art practice is "diversity of tactics," the same slogan that anti-globalization activists have mobilized to overcome divisions of political orientation. In this, it is not always possible to distinguish engaged, anti-capitalist art from contemporary, post-political vanguardism, as gender and race issues, for example, or as anarchist and Marxist tendencies vie for political prominence.

The tendencies that I am concerned with here are influenced by strategies that resemble those that are used in protest aesthetics. Theoretical tensions within the movement often arise around the concept of autonomy, which has, on the one hand, a political sense related to notions of self-organization, collectivity, and solidarity, and on the other, a theoretical sense that is both philosophical and socio-historical. Diversity of tactics emphasizes a logic of affinity that binds networks of grassroots organizations whose decentralized structures reflect both a political outlook and a means to resist state repression. These principles are advocated by the collective Chto Delat, who state the importance of twentieth-century avant-garde thought for the renewal of leftist organization, and for a nondogmatic approach to Marxism based in the principles of internationalism, feminism, and equality.[8] Tactics aside, it is necessary to assert that particularisms of gender, race, and sexuality are equally mediated by capital and that in neoliberal society, the struggle against capital has made identity struggles a matter of political formality. David Graeber makes the observation that the struggle against oppression is complemented by the struggle against alienation and that no amount of political correctness can quench the thirst for a universal emancipation.[9]

Les pauvres vont pas voir de shows/Icitte, l'hiver, les pauvres gèlent

In 2008, on the ten-year anniversary of ATSA's first version of *État d'Urgence* (*EU*), the group was awarded two major municipal awards by the City of Montreal: *Artistes pour la paix* (Artists for Peace) and *Citoyen de la Culture* (Cultural Citizen). The prizes recognized the tenacity of the artists in sustaining their annual urban refugee camp on the Place Émilie-Gamelin, a five-day "manifestival" that offers the public artistic programming that showcases problems related to homelessness and social exclusion. *EU*'s focus on homelessness corresponds to ATSA's "terrorist" strategy of creating attention-grabbing urban guerrilla art aimed at various ecosocial ills, including poverty, consumerism and environmental degradation. For the 2009 version of *État d'Urgence*, I spent five days observing some of the countless activities that were organized. In the following I describe these wanderings with a view to placing ATSA's *État d'Urgence* in the context of homeless representation. The program was titled *Hygiène sociale* (Social Hygiene), a means of addressing the media-generated hysterics surrounding the H1N1 flu virus, and redirecting attention towards the stigma surrounding vagrancy. For the first time, ATSA partnered with Amnesty International to bring attention to poverty and homelessness as human rights issues.

Whereas the 1997 *Banque à bas* (which translates roughly into Sock Bank or Down with Banks) started as a discrete sculptural provocation, "plunked" on the doorstep of the Montreal Musée d'art contemporain, its *EU* offshoot has grown exponentially.[10] In 2009, it had numerous government partners, including Heritage Canada, the Canada Council, the Government of Québec (Conseil des arts et des lettres, Emploi Québec, Ministère des affaires municipales), the City of Montreal, the Conseil des Arts de Montréal, and the real estate consortium La Capitale. It had over thirty business partners in the areas of communications, advertising, cultural promotion, and transportation. In addition, the *EU* website lists an impressive number of collaborators in logistics, restaurants, promotion and graphic design, personal care, food donation, clothing donation, fair trade, artistic support, a hotel for visiting artists, and bingo volunteers.[11] The ATSA team included a general coordinator, production assistant, coordination assistant, promotion agent, accountant, webmasters, photographer, translator, video editor, four artistic advisors, and six board governors. With all of this support, ATSA's Allard and Roy can very well be described as impresarios, bridging activism and popular art.[12] The success of the project as a spectacular humanitarian effort has caused it to grow over the years with volunteers now numbering over four hundred, the number of meals doubling to approximately two hundred fifty three times daily, and the number of participating artists over the one hundred mark. Any polemical stance directed at ATSA's attention-grabbing strategies has therefore to address the immense popularity of this annual event. The festival features five days of continuous and free multidisciplinary artistic presentations, including circus, theater, visual arts, video, film, spoken word, storytelling, comedy, music, and dance. *EU* provides warm clothing, over thirty-five hundred meals, snacks, sleeping accommodations, and health and beauty services. For these five days, the Place Émilie-Gamelin becomes a meeting place for street people who mingle with spectators.

According to Louis Jacob, the key characteristic of ATSA's interventionist strategy is participation, a transformative experience of dialogue and interaction.[13] The openness of the project is due not only to the fact it is oriented to the general public and non-specialized, non-art audiences, but that people are free to come and go, with the only restrictions being the cold weather and occasional rain or snow. In this provisional space of emergency rescue through communication and community, there appear to be no exceptions. It is worth mentioning that the first versions of *EU* were designed to provide the general public with the experience of sleeping in a makeshift shelter and relying on food rations rather than the comforts of home. The audience that turned out for these first few projects, however, consisted mostly of homeless people who needed the services that were intended to be primarily symbolic. Since then, *EU* has both adopted its core constituency and adapted its methods of organization in order to spread its message as broadly as possible.

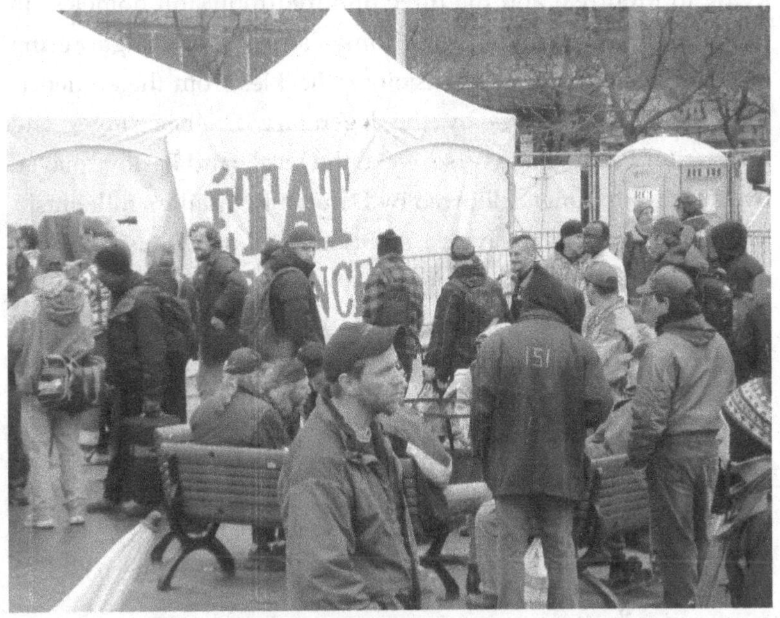

ATSA, *État d'Urgence*, 2009. Place Émilie-Gamelin, Montreal.
Photo: Marc James Léger.

November 25: On va l'avoir

On Friday, in the light rain of a cold fall evening, I went to see *Le Show Hygiénique*, hosted by Sylvie Moreau and François Papineau. Approximately one hundred people had gathered, some sitting on benches that had been placed around metal drums with lit fires. There were indications that this was a night of some excitement, with the smell of pot in the air and people huddled about, holding beer cans in brown paper bags. I met two young men in the Amnesty International tent who were working on a campaign for Paraguay that they linked to their anti-poverty campaign for Québec. Then the show started. The hosts wore white lab coats and the musicians wore blue hospital gowns. Moreau and Papineau insisted ironically that the event was not politically partisan and then proceeded to provide statistics concerning the ten to fifteen thousand homeless people living in Montréal and the three hundred thousand homeless in Canada. Their banter was funny and twisted, garnering favourable and sometimes disjointed heckles from the audience. They sang *Les Pauvres* by the legendary Québec singer and songwriter Plume Latraverse. Next, the local band Parlovr played two synth-pop tunes, followed by Damien Robitaille's folk music, Mathieu Lippé's slam lyrics, and some country music. People danced by the stage and one man took the microphone, letting out an assertive, existential scream. Before the show was over I bought from the welcome tent a copy of ATSA's self-published book, *ATSA: Quand l'art passe à l'action* (ATSA: When Art Takes Action). The title brings to mind the action art of the 1960s and the development of performance art. One art action, you could say, was enacted by a young woman named Julie who decided during the show that I was going to share my umbrella with her. *"Il faut partager,"* she said; "you have to share."

November 26: I Heart Joseph Beuys

The following morning, on the way to the camp, I met a man on Saint-Denis Street who was selling the homeless newsmagazine *L'Itinéraire*. He said he likes to keep a low profile and thought that *EU* is a bit too showy and spectacular, that people like him need health services and beds, delivered in a calm and secure environment. He spoke to me about having a bipolar disorder and suffering from depression. I thought to myself, the entire world today suffers from these same problems. Remembering some things I learned from studying the work of Krzysztof Wodiczko, I told him that I hoped the show on Saint-Catherine would help all of us learn to live a little. He smiled and shook my hand.

I strolled onto the plaza where the night before some one hundred people had slept. People were now lined up at the food tents. I spoke for a while to Marie-Pierre, a security volunteer who said somewhat apologetically that things had gotten rowdy last night. She then explained that Montreal shelters cannot provide beds for all of the people in need. The overflow that ATSA serves is a spectacular reminder that there aren't enough beds to meet the demand. She said that if I wanted to know more I should mingle with the people. As I walked towards a nearby café to read the articles on ATSA in the issue of *L'Itinéraire* that I bought, I fell upon a silent performance by a group of young people. These anonymous individuals held their various poses in front of Jean-François Lemire's outdoor photo installation, a series of banners with portraits of people who may or may not be homeless. During the performance a young street person named Christian explained to me that the insurance costs from theft are an unnecessary expense and that a free-market solution to homelessness is readily at hand for entrepreneurs who could receive subsidies by providing "private" housing. This he believed could help cut down on crime and maybe drug abuse. At the coffee shop, two steps away from the plaza, the tables have signs glued to them that are printed by the Montreal police. The signs remind customers to watch their things: "Theft doesn't take a break." Obviously, Christian is aware that theft has causes and is not an impersonal, timeless evil.[14] The manager of the café was unclear about what was going on across the street. When I explained things to her she said she thought that perhaps the money could be put to better use and that the festival might not be for everybody.

Later, in the ATSA tent, Anne Ste-Marie from Amnesty International gave a media conference on the First Nations Winneway community in central Québec. She related the contemporary conditions of this Algonquin group to the history of European colonialism. Ten percent of itinerants in Canada, she explained, are native people. Natives are poorer than the average poor Canadian, have a lower life expectancy, and receive 28 percent less in terms of services. She explained how the Long

Point First Nation's efforts to control its economic development, territory, and ancestral lands, named Kakinwawigak, are typically caught between provincial and federal legislation. Since the government of Prime Minister Stephen Harper is closed to discussion, Amnesty is focusing its energy on the provincial administration of Jean Charest, premier of Québec. She passed out postcards to the people in the tent, who were lined up for coffee and Christmas cake and benefiting from services from Médecins du monde, an anonymous barber, the used clothing seller Value Village, and the Patchwork Workshop. While I was sitting on the barber's empty chair, a woman showed me the fur coat she had claimed from Value Village. "It's full of holes," she told me. "You can take it to the mending booth," I suggested. She just smiled and got along in the snack lineup. Later, after the conference was over, I saw her wearing the coat.

My Thursday at *EU* was rounded off with an artist's talk at the Goethe Institut on Sherbrooke Street. ATSA had met Hans Winkler at an event in Vancouver and invited him to participate in this year's programming. This international artist, who is now based in New York City, makes interventionist works that create occasions for social interactions in urban contexts. His piece for *EU* is a projected handbook with tips and survival strategies gathered while "in residence." Not only is the handbook based on the expertise of Montreal's homeless people and drug addicts, it carries the fearful prospect that it could become a handy reference for anyone in today's world of economic instability. Some of the tips he has been given, he says, are little more than "bullshit." I asked Winkler who his influences were. He emphasized Dada, Futurism, and the Flux artists Wolf Vostell and Joseph Beuys. The Futurism accounts for his occasional forays into the realm of illegality. When I pressed him on the stakes of contemporary criticism related to engaged art, he said with a blasé attitude: "Yeah, people were talking a lot about avant-garde ten years ago."

November 27: Devenir itinérant

At lunch on Friday I attended the lecture given by Université du Québec à Montréal professor Simon Harel at the Bibliothèque Nationale on Berri Street, situated diagonally across from Place Émilie-Gamelin. Harel is director of the University's *Centre interuniversitaire d'étude sur les lettres, les arts et les traditions*. He spoke in particular of the Place Émilie-Gamelin as part of the underground manifestations of Québec culture, bordering the popular and commercial Quartier des Spectacles that is best known for the annual summer jazz festival. The survival of public places like the Place Émilie-Gamelin depends on the city preventing such sites from becoming the kind of museological zones that characterize Venice and Bilbao. It is an example of a park that works for its users, a site of reappropriation of the city by itinerants. Montreal's future, he argued, lies in remaining an alternative city in which such places are still a possibility. He said that the city has to avoid what Michael Sorkin refers to as "domestication by cappuccino."[15] Literature, Harel argued, is another of the sites in which the marginal culture of Montreal is valorized, and ATSA, he insisted, *is* Montreal.

Harel's talk about an imaginary of rebellion amongst the city's "children of the streets," about the language of wandering and desperate nomadism, was lost on a local advocate of police and municipal intervention to "clean up" the plaza from drug dealers. This man thought that Harel was romanticizing the street and rowdy users of the park. I also thought that Harel was glorifying itinerance, but not in the same sense. Montreal underground is significant to Harel inasmuch as it serves Québécois identity. Not a word was spoken about class struggle as an international project and the kinds of effort required to eliminate poverty and unemployment.[16] While the savoir-faire of survival and solidarity strategies are undoubtedly local, Harel limits his discourse to the kind of incremental reformism that ignores the relative impossibility of capitalism with a human face within the current political climate. He could have been reminded that the politics of the 1960s, of which he spoke, was also a class politics. No one in the room seemed to understand that Bilbaoization serves mostly reified cultural projects. Harel did not articulate an alternative global vision but an alternative neoliberalism.

November 28: L'amour fou

On Saturday I decided to see the play *Ça va la santé mentale?* (How's Your Mental Health?). I confused the stages, however, and listened instead to the choral music of *Les Voix Ferrées*. By day four, the crowd had grown a little irreverent. Although I took a seat at the back of the scene, I was surrounded in a few minutes by distracted participants, a man playing his guitar, photographers shooting by the minute, and a group of homeless men with big dogs. Part of the spectacle sometimes provided by homeless people is their disrespect for the conventions of civility. They make noise during shows, spit on the ground, and talk back to emcees in ways that redirect the show towards idiosyncratic ends.

In the evening I saw Magnus Isaacson and Simon Bujold's recent documentary, *L'Art en action: Un film sur ATSA* (Canada, 2009, Isaacson and Bujold). This presentation at the Cinéma Parallèle was not part of the official selection for the festival, but the timing could not have been better. The film looks at the work of Allard and Roy over ten years. Among one of the insights of the film is the way that the artists mix political sophistication with a forthrightness that is characteristic of Montrealers. Roy is shown crying at least three times in the film, sometimes of fatigue and other times of frustration concerning the dire circumstances of the people she meets.

One of the scenes from the 2008 *EU* shows the two artists greeting the mayor, Gerald Tremblay, on the big stage. Tremblay is treated to the projected video image of an advocate for the homeless who explains how in the past year, city police have awarded more than four thousand fines to homeless people. The mayor tells the assembled that he is aware of this criminalization of poverty and says that his administration is looking into the issue. Allard confronts him somewhat menacingly while Roy puts her arm around him reassuringly. Allard is not always easy to handle. More than anything, they tell their interviewer, ATSA is about energy, the love of wild things, the unfinished. The film culminates with the closing of *EU* 2008 wherein the children of the Arc-en-ciel primary school, who have been serving meals all night, finish their duties by singing John Lennon's "Imagine."[17] After weeks of tireless organizing and days of intense interaction with Montreal's homeless, Roy is moved once again to tears.

November 29: L'Amour ça se fout

On Sunday, the last day of events, I attend the dance training session presented by La 2e Porte à gauche (Second Door on the Left), a group influenced by Michel Reilhac's Bal Moderne and whose members presented to the public Marie Chouinard's choreography for *Orpheus and Euridice*. About twenty people from the crowd joined in to learn the dance steps. On each side of the stage are huge illustrated banners by Donigan Cumming. Called *Kincora*, the drawings were inspired by a scandalous eviction that put out hundreds of people. The participants learned the steps after about a dozen or so attempts and entertained everyone else in the process.

My penchant for cinema later brought me to another film screening, this one presented at the National Film Board on Saint-Denis Street. *50-10 Un toit, c'est un droit* (Canada, 2008, Vera-Villaneuva) is a documentary made by ATSA's neighbour, Henrique Vera-Villanueva. It depicts the 2008 *EU* in what the filmmaker, who was in attendance at the screening, describes as a photograph of the event. The film's title marks the passage of sixty years of the Human Rights Declaration and ten years of *État d'Urgence*. One of the songs featured in the sound track intones:

"L'amour ça se fout d'être amant" (Love doesn't bother to be in love). The song doubles ATSA's art, which doesn't bother being aesthetic. Artists are depicted as well as political groups, including representatives from the newly created provincial party Québec Solidaire and the Ontario Coalition Against Poverty. The same interlude with the mayor that was featured in *L'Art en action* appears in this film. One man who was interviewed explained how a fine prevented him from getting off of police parole and getting a desirable job. I met the director after the screening. He let me know that a bill to reform the business of fines awarded to the homeless had made it to a superior court.

From Universal Rights to Universal Exception

The month of November 2009 in which this edition of *État d'Urgence* took place marked the anniversary of two major world-historical events: the "fall of the Berlin Wall" in 1989 and the confrontation of anti-global activists against the World Trade Organization summit in Seattle in 1999. Both events signaled a new era, and both of them met immediate setbacks. The former Soviet-bloc countries did not see a new era of freedoms and opportunities arise, but the return of former Communists to positions of power within a neoliberal "risk society" that does not have any of the previous guarantees of social welfare. After Seattle, the post-9/11 "criminalization of dissent" and the repressive police force used against anti-globalization protesters in Genoa brought with it a certain realization of the systemic antagonisms of biocapitalist governmentality. If these anniversaries have been noteworthy, it is in allowing us to take stock of the present conjuncture. As Slavoj Žižek argued,

November 1989 marked the beginning of the "happy 1990s," Francis Fukuyama's utopian "end of history": liberal democracy, he announced, had effectively won, the advent of a global, liberal world community lurked just around the corner, and the remaining obstacles to this happy ending were merely contingent (pockets of resistance where the local leaders hadn't yet grasped that their day was done). In contrast, 9/11 marked the symbolic end of the "happy 1990s": it signaled the beginning of our current era, in which new walls are springing up everywhere, between Israel and the West Bank, around the European Union, on the US-Mexico border – but also within single states.[18]

Žižek argues that 9/11 and the 2008 economic meltdown represent the collapse of the Fukuyaman utopia of liberal-democratic politics. What do we have in its place? What can be observed in Canada under Stephen Harper, in the United States under Barack Obama, and in European countries under the EU is the progressive disappearance of a leftist option, of anything that resembles welfare-state social democracy. Instead, in the new "post-political" situation, the option is between a mainstream, politically correct liberal capitalism and a rightist, populist reaction to it. Whatever remains of the left, he argues, is so terrified of using the language of class struggle that most spend their time convincing themselves that the left is the party of the new postmodern, digital capitalism.[19]

Two points can be derived from Žižek's argument that have implications for how we view materialist art practices that address social issues like homelessness. Both of these have to do with the way we conceive postmodernism in relation to leftist discourse. In her introductory essay to the book project that accompanied her 1991 exhibition, *If You Lived Here*, Martha Rosler made the following assertion: "The dead hand of 'universalism' has lain heavily on documentary's shoulder, for a documentary work alibied as revealing an underlying human sameness becomes simply an excuse for spectacle."[20] Similar anti-universalist views were the basis of writings like those of Rosalyn Deutsche, who referred to Ernesto Laclau and Chantal

Mouffe's theory of radical democracy to account for the ways that power is always in the process of being hegemonized but can never be ideologically consistent. In the course of the last decade, however, the postmodern politics of cultural difference have been reevaluated according to anti-essentialist theories of struggle and emancipation that have revised the postmodern critique of universality.[21] Taking universality into account, the poor and the homeless are not so much an ontological, specifiable group of people, but a figure of the inherent divisibility of the social, a condition of capitalism's self-relating as the concrete universal. The homeless are not outside capitalism but represent the "universal exception," a limit case against which the general, universal capitalist condition is understood. If the global proletariat cannot be directly invoked in the context of a global city like Montreal, then the homeless are certainly part of that class as the inherent split against which it is impossible to consider the existing political order to be democratic.[22] The conservative formula, here as elsewhere, is to individualize social problems.

From this perspective, it is possible to rethink the "identificatory" practices of documentary photography and similar "socially concerned" art practices – not from the point of view of a critique of liberal humanism, however, but as part of a contemporary critique of neoliberal post-politics. Related to this is a second point about postmodern theorizing. It is clear that some segments of today's anti-global or alter-global left identify with the postmodern critique of meta-narratives and the view that revolutionary struggle cannot overcome the contradictions of capital. The concept of "multitude," for instance, has for some people replaced class analysis as the social basis of resistance to post-Fordist forms of discipline.[23]

One outcome of the emergence of the movement of the multitude is the articulation of a new set of politics around the terms "precarity," "precarization," and "precariat." According to Hal Foster, no concept better comprehends the art of the 2000s than that which is termed "precarious."[24] Without a doubt, some aspects of the *Oxford English Dictionary* definition of precarious that Foster highlights can be said to correspond to ATSA's *État d'Urgence*: obtained by entreaty; depending on the favour of another; social state of insecurity; mournful and desperate; attesting to the violence done to basic principles of human responsibility.[25] Gerald Raunig, for his part, invokes the use of the term by the Milanese precarity movement in contrast to the etymological usage in its passive form, which implies victimization.[26] Since 2001 and following the G8 summit in Genoa, the Milanese and Barcelona Mayday parades have mobilized a "generation of the precarious," leading to meetings in cities across Europe and to the development of "living wage" policy concepts like "flexicurity," a form of social insurance for the precarious creative worker of the new post-Fordist economy. Whereas one might argue that the precariat, digitariat, and cognitariat represent privileged sectors of society, the notion of multitude resists the logic of identity and classification that leads to class competitiveness. The anti-identitary form of the precariat, Raunig argues, is a matter of self-representation and constituent power, emphasizing the intercourse of differences more than unity.

The upshot of struggles between socialist and anarchist tendencies on the left implies, minimally, that criticism of engaged art practice has a basis in radical politics.[27] Perhaps the most radical critique of engaged cultural praxis has been put forward by the collective BAVO, which argues that artists should resist the demand made by neoliberal capitalism for artists in the post-welfare state to take up the role of the "last of the idealists."[28] The kinds of ameliorative critique that are allowed by capitalism are the kinds that do not call into question the functioning of the system itself. Engaged art practices have become increasingly ineffective, the collective argues, inasmuch as they conform to what is demanded of artists. BAVO states:

This societal demand is, in fact, a bogus one, since art's critical or utopian mandate is simultaneously limited to the constant warning that its activity should remain realistic and especially constructive. Such constructive criticism is, of course, nothing but a coded way of saying that it should not question or undermine the win-win combination of representative democracy and free market economy – the two "golden calves" of this self-acclaimed age of the end of history. If artists *do* get carried away by their iconoclastic or revolutionary enthusiasm, they are immediately accused of regressing into backward, totalitarian forms of society, preaching anarchy or even paving the way for terrorism.[29]

Of course, people in grassroots democracy movements accuse governments of the same nostalgia for nineteenth-century laissez-faire ideology as well as the totalitarian orchestration of oligarchic politics. The chant "George Bush, Terrorist" was commonly heard at social justice and antiwar protests during the Bush years.[30] At every stage, however, the activist logic of intervention is countered by the placid, self-assured interference of neoliberals. In 1997, for example, Stephen Harper stated that conservatives should "work to dismantle the remaining elements of the interventionist state," a view that is inherent to his administration's efforts to privatize public services.[31]

As a very important first stage in the process of dissolving identification with, on the one hand, the state institutions that merely look for legitimization from activists and NGOs, and on the other, the art institutions that have delivered us to the postmodern no-man's-land beyond left and right, ATSA's *État d'Urgence* points to the symptomatic aspects of socially ameliorative activism. In this, ATSA's work has the merit of revealing the repressed element in art's reconciliation with its capitalist functions, namely, art's radical potential. *État d'Urgence* achieves this "traversal" of the alienating activity of art by organizing an encounter of the precarious. Paradoxically, this encounter is densely mediated by the work of numerous artists and performers, artists who may or may not be thinking about the ideology that structures so much of their activity.

The Non-Productive Role of the Artist: The Creative Industries in Canada

We say that creative industries are an enormous part of our country's future... I say we give them a fair shake and treat them as the entrepreneurs and small business owners they are.
– Jack Layton, former leader of the New Democratic Party

There's an incredible economic trickle-down effect to the arts in this country and you cannot dismiss it as being something we watch in the glamorous events.
– Atom Egoyan, filmmaker

In October of 2008, on the corner of Laval Avenue and Duluth, one of Montreal's anonymous graffiti artists posted a wheatpaste stencil of Canadian Prime Minister Stephen Harper. Harper is depicted playing his piano, as was seen on television reports in the days leading to the Fall elections. The image conjures a singer songwriter blending political banter with finger play: "... I think when ordinary working people come home... and they turn on the TV and see a bunch of people at a rich gala... all subsidised by taxpayers.... I'm not sure that's something that r-e-s-o-n-a-t-e-s with ordinary people..." For whatever reason, this wonderful piece, a rare treat in a town of tiresome graffiti scribblings, was destroyed in a matter of days.

For those artists and artists' representation groups that came together in September 2008 to protest the Canadian Conservative government's cuts to arts funding and the attacks on cultural producers whose activities are deemed "outside the mainstream" and therefore "the national interest," Harper's piano playing will not soon be forgotten. His televised presentation of the private pleasures of piano playing came at the time of the televised parliamentary leaders' debates of October 1 and 2, 2008. His effort to present himself as a liberal humanist was accompanied by explanations that the cuts (to PromArt, the Canadian Memory Fund, Canadian Culture Online, Audio Visual Trust, Film and Video Fund, Trade Routes and Aboriginal Peoples' TV Network) were not motivated by political considerations, but by cost accounting. "There's no ideological agenda there," he stated.

The cuts to arts funding were announced just before the October 2008 federal election debates and we can assume from this that the Harper conservatives expected their baiting of the "elite" cultural sector to find a receptive audience among ordinary Canadians. The policy options that were presented to the electoral public at this time provide an indication of what cultural policies are imaginable at the level of Canadian federal politics, and as such, what Canadians and *Québecois* can expect in the years ahead. While an idealistic argument might make a claim for a reconsideration of the role of the artist, either in terms of community leadership, or more naively, as leading Canadians in the global challenge of creative competition, I think it is better to try to understand the curious position artists find themselves in now that government and business are interested in the commercial potential of art and culture, and from there, think through our roles in mediating the political economy of contemporary cultural production.

Economic growth is today associated with creativity. To take a typical example, one of the current slogans of the Royal Bank of Canada states: "What do you want to create?" Next to the neoliberal fantasy that culture may someday help to make up for declining rates of profit is a more fundamental question having to do with the power of transnational corporations to impose change on all aspects of human existence. For good and bad, cultural production, associated with creative thinking and innovation, has been conflated with new industries, mostly in the area of communications technology, and deemed a catalyst for economic growth. The name that neoliberal policy makers have given to this new approach to cultural administration is the *creative industries*. The last few years have witnessed a still emergent, yet widespread critique of creative industries discourse. While there is no official position on the creative industries in the Canadian context, and certainly nothing like that established by the Blair government in the U.K., I argue that a creative industries mindset, without being named as such, is in effect at the level of Canadian federal cultural policy.

In her 2008 essay on "Crude Culture," Kirsty Robertson argued in the pages of *Fuse* magazine that Canadians typically respond with incredulity to the amalgamation of culture and the economy.[1] In this, the first serious treatment of creative industries discourse as it relates to Canada, Robertson notes that this subject was not even raised by the attendees of the 2007 Visual Arts Summit in Ottawa, the first major gathering of visual arts professionals since the 1951 Massey Commission.[2] She states that the kind of boosterism that links culture and technology with the global economy is largely absent in Canada and the reasons for this have to do with the identity debates of the 1990s, which pit federalists against Québec nationalists and First Nations peoples, and which thus distinguish Canada from other G8 nations. Seeking to make a properly cultural argument for the need to think creatively about the creative industries, Robertson ignores the dynamics that characterize Canadian economic growth.

Jim Stanford, a noted economist with the Canadian Auto Workers union, argues that not only is Canada's relatively small economy largely dependent on resource extraction, but that its small internal markets tend to undermine innovative activity and rely on foreign ownership.[3] While identity issues may very well accompany the protectionism of prominent left nationalists like Maude Barlow and Mel Watkins, as Robertson argues, my view is that *political* autonomy is their chief motivating factor, and that here, paradoxically, art and politics are only incidentally conflated. What is missing in Robertson's essay is a critical analysis of the politics that mediate both culture and the economy. In other words, what we need is not only a socially progressive articulation of the links between culture, technology and the global economy, but a critique of the political economy of neoliberal cultural production that is able to politicize cultural value and cultural meaning rather than culturalize politics. Watkins and Barlow are more than correct to identify with citizens' movements across the globe who resist the neoliberal agenda, and do so because they recognize that cultural production, like other forms of industry, is not free from state regulation, and as such, from ideological pressures. Rather than ignore the state regulation of culture, a radical analysis of cultural production should meet it head on. One preliminary observation concerning the contradictions of liberal capitalism is that economic growth does not necessarily entail social progress. Industrial growth has been shown to lead in most cases to capital accumulation, with increased economic disparity among classes as well as a worsening of conditions for those most disadvantaged.

In his four-volume treatise on the "statist mode of production," Henri Lefebvre argued that the modern state abandons the political concept of progress in favour of the ideology of economic growth, which creates crises between the relatively autonomous sphere of the economic and the sphere of culture.[4] Inasmuch as contemporary analysis of the creative industries has placed a great deal of emphasis on creative or immaterial labour and the knowledge production of the "general intellect," it becomes all the more difficult to think of social relations and post-Fordist modes of production as directly cultural. The near absence of any serious discussion of the culture industries in Canada, let alone of any resistance to it, is only apparent, however, since cultural identities are precisely the vehicles through which Canadians have been taught and teach themselves to misperceive the link between culture and economic domination. What else could creative industry policies represent for Canadians than that which David Morley and Kevin Robins described in the late 1980s as "Canadianization," a term that was once used internationally to define the transformation of national cultures brought about by trade liberalization and communications technologies?[5] More recently, Bill Readings asked us to consider whether or not the institutions of Canadian art – even when they are publicly funded – serve any purpose outside of transnational globalization.[6]

The sustaining myths of this colonial dilemma, as I have called it, have been apologetic narratives of a properly Canadian and/or Québécois experience, supplemented with postmodern attention to First Nations as part of a broader agenda of tolerance towards cultural diversity.[7] Since the identity politics of the 1980s, cultural identity has also focused on issues related to feminist politics, antiracism and queer practice. Our attention to the contradictions of culture should nevertheless begin by recognizing Canada's privileged place among the G7 nations and within the Quad of the World Trade Organization. In this conjuncture, the protection and promotion of identities (through both high art and popular culture) and the privatization agenda (culture and creativity as a new area for investment) can be seen to work in tandem. The radical philosopher Alain Badiou argues that identity should be separated from the state.[8] We should add to this art and culture. Art should be separate from the state, not for the sake of protecting creative expression, but because of the ways it reveals of the incompleteness of politics.

Ordinary Citizens in an Ordinary Industry

A spectacular exposé of the state of federal policy in the area of cultural production could be gleaned from the Canadian parliamentary leaders' debates of October 2008.[9] More significant than the policies of any one political party, this gathering of party leaders provided an indication of what cultural policies are imaginable at the level of Canadian federal politics. The unstated premise of the debate, the neoliberal engineering of culture, had been surreptitiously "leaked" with the August announcement by the Conservative government under Stephen Harper that $45M in arts funding would be cut inasmuch as it supported economically ineffective programs, not to mention a number of small grants to what the Conservatives considered to be "highly ideological individuals exposing their agendas."[10] The Prime Minister's remarks were aimed at the recipients of grants from the PromArt program which provided travel funds to artists. Of the $4.7 million budget allocated to PromArt, Harper singled out small grants that had gone to "radicals," "left-wing and anti-globalization think tanks," and "ideological activists or fringe and alternative groups."[11]

Paradoxically, this neoconservative excess, correctly identified by Bloc Québécois leader Gilles Duceppe as a moral position, and by Green Party leader Elizabeth May as a mean spirited means to garner favour with the populist electorate, allowed the Bloc, the Greens, the New Democratic Party and the Liberal Party to counter Harper with different versions of free market ideology. The opposition leaders unanimously underscored art's contribution to investment and economic activity. May supported her position by citing the research of Richard Florida and his theory of the creative class. In addition, the leaders put forward their particular party's pluralist vision of identity formation, either promising Québecers a meaningful nationalism (Duceppe), or Canadians "more fun" expressing themselves and distinguishing themselves from the United States (former Liberal leader Stéphane Dion). Viewpoints similar to these had been expressed in September when various artists' groups rallied to condemn the cuts as economically short-sighted. Richard Hardacre, the National President of the performers' guild ACTRA, reminded the press that according to the Conference Board of Canada, the more than one million Canadians who work in the culture industries produce an annual value of $86B (7.5%) in GDP. The conservative *National Post* later reported anxiously on the elasticity of the term culture industry, noting that the correct figure was $84.6B and that the largest component of the direct gains from sales came from the advertising industry.[12]

The tipping point in the culture segment of the election debate came with NDP leader Jack Layton's rebuttal to the Conservatives that most artists, making an average $10-12,000 per year, would not have much use for their proposed $500 tax incentive for children's enrollments in art activities (like piano lessons) if these same families cannot afford them. Beyond the promise of more funding, since, as he said, "you get more leverage [with the arts] than in any other sector of the economy," and beyond the recommendation of serious tax breaks to artists instead of banks, Layton added that the Harper cuts limit the freedom of those who express controversial ideas. Just as Canada's competitors are eagerly finding ways to get "huge returns on investment in the arts" (Layton), the opposition parties seemed to be saying, the Conservative government makes use of both liberal elitism and working-class populism to mystify cost-accounting and vice versa.

The problem here of course is that the late NDP leader did little more than emphasize the demands of global market capitalism. How are we to understand the contradictions of these demands if culture is meant to assert identity within a transnational process of symbolic production, and, alternately, if global post-industrial processes make its producers "ordinary workers" and small-time entrepreneurs, and not, as conservative discourse would have it, a decadent elite, dependent on state subsidies? What is clear from this debate is that it is virtually impossible for any of Canada's political party leaders to construct a view of art's social function as being anything other than a gauge of economic productivity and competitiveness, on the one hand, or a cipher for liberal pluralism. The emphasis that they like to place on identity is more than a convenient alibi for economic restructuring, it is a direct indication of their inability or unwillingness to address art's contribution to the reproduction of capitalist class relations. This failure indicates a further inability to conceive of a global social movement able to confront market logic with new models of social cooperation that link the conditions of work to social justice.

The manner in which Canadian cultural organizations have responded to Finance Minister Jim Flaherty's 2009 Conservative budget might offer an occasion to table a provisional answer to the question raised by Robertson: Why is there so little discussion of the creative industries in Canada? Robertson wonders if the Canadian penchant for public funding as a means to protect Canadian identity and jobs can be mobilized as an oppositional discourse against the neoliberal engineering of art and culture through capital investment and marketization. Identities, ostensibly the key feature of social struggle, seem to be in good enough care since there were no major budget cuts in the Spring of 2009 in what Alain Pineau, National Director of the Canadian Conference of the Arts, has called a status quo budget. (But then, when it comes to identities, isn't this always the case? Not so for jobs.) Although the arts, he says, have not been factored in as a significant stimulus to the flagging economy, there were no major cuts either and some significant infrastructure funding has gone to building a positive relationship with the arts sector. Despite the knowledge that the culture industries represent a significant portion of the national GDP, individuals, organizations and institutions that are accustomed to receiving a significant proportion of their budget from government subsidies and grants find themselves in the awkward position of having to account for their new role as economic stimulants. After all, is the field of cultural production, as Pierre Bourdieu argued, not supposed to be characterized by an inversion of the economic interests that motivate other sectors of society? And does Harper's assertion that "art is a part of my soul" not play to idealist and romantic notions of aestheticism better than talk of a creative class, which may sound to untrained ears more like socialism and sociology than the liberal arts? Notwithstanding the plethora of atavisms available to spin doctors, art professionals are correct to pressure their governments to recognize and respect their political wishes. As actor Art Hindle stated at the time of the September cuts, the art industry, like other sectors of the economy, more than pays its way.

The kinds of changes that the creative industries model adopted by the British government imposes on contemporary artists involves an emphasis on heritage and the brokering of identities as the main object of exchange in international tourism and cultural consumption, the confusion of cultural and academic knowledge production with the high-tech sector for the sake of profit, and the conflation of culture with competitive sport. According to the Glasgow-based online journal *Variant*, a bill to transform the Scottish Arts Council and Scottish Screen into a single, private company was defeated in 2003. The next year, Scotland's Labour Party launched a Cultural Commission to further influence future cultural policy in the direction of Creative Scotland. In February of 2008, a convention titled "Scotland: Creative Nation, Cultural Summit," was attended by Charles Leadbeater, the architect of the British Creative Industries model. The Summit further encouraged the integration of cultural policy with the creation of economic wealth. Reporting critically on these processes, *Variant* was threatened with legal action by Culture and Sport Glasgow for "defamatory statements."[13] In 2012, government cuts have effectively silenced the magazine. We have here the key ingredient to what Robertson correctly identifies as the unspoken and unidentified possibility of a creative industry policy shift in Canada:

intimidation. Along these lines – a privatization and vocational-ization of culture similar to that imposed on higher education – we can imagine a future wherein the Canada Council will operate as a corporation, artists will be awarded loans instead of grants, conservative bureaucrats will wait out and starve dissenting voices, and statistics and market indicators will rule the day as instruments to be used to determine the kind of work that should be made, and indeed, who we are and what we are to become. The effort to regulate the content of a progressive culture and politics magazine like *Variant* should provide us with a clue to what remains unspoken in much of the Canadian art scene: the post-political view that neoliberalism and ever more authoritarian forms of capitalism set the political agenda.

The contradictions of the capitalist emphasis on growth and productivity affect progressive cultural workers through both the recuperation of avant-garde cultural experimentation and the disciplining of radical cultural expression. One of the most egregious cases of the latter is the prosecution by the U.S. Department of Justice of artist Steve Kurtz and scientist Robert Ferrell for their work with Critical Art Ensemble on *Free Range Grain*, a harmless do-it-yourself analysis of bioengineering.[14] Another example is the 2007 arrest, interrogation and detainment of sociology professor Andrej Holm by the German federal police. Holm, who happened to be a participant in the demonstrations against the World Economic Summit in Heiligendamm, was detained because his publications contained words like inequality, precarization and gentrification, words that were deemed by police to be the kind of language used by militant terrorist organizations.[15] If the civil liberties of artists and sociologists producing politically-motivated work can be so easily revoked through repressive state action, it is partly because political power is distributed anonymously across all social institutions. One should be careful not to overstate the function of disciplinary state security, however, since the purpose of neoliberal governments is largely to produce self-interested individuals who can act autonomously within market relations of inequality. The risks of exclusion and discipline are part of the generalized management of critique and creativity that drives today's corporate sector mentality. Critical work now comes under new kinds of institutional pressure. Not only must artists continue to justify the relevance of theory to practice, they must constantly justify the political salience of cultural work as such, a fact that tends to deliver art over to capitalist social engineering.[16]

Creative Confusion

The conditions of cultural production that prevail within advanced capitalist countries like Canada require that contemporary artists think about the demands that are made by neoliberal market capitalism for the creative production of new symbols and new knowledges. The main problem that confronts contemporary artists is the way that the creative industries are based in an apparent distinction between production and the capitalization of markets. We can easily link the question of demand to the problem of cultural production as a form of subjective destitution. The work of the vast majority of artists, sustained by the desire for social mobility, economic reward and cultural consecration, is alienated by the symbolic authority of the demand. The realization of this means to treat oneself as an object of technocratic administration, a condition in which the supply of creative services, information, affect and experience addresses producers as rational, self-regulating and entrepreneurial individuals who condition themselves according to norms of production that minimize risk and maximize self-interest.

The post-operaist thinker Maurizio Lazzarato explains the new forms of biopolitical administration in terms of structural changes to the labour market, introduced primarily by the state.

Market capitalism transforms artists into "workers," a hybrid of employer and employee, and thus into "human capital" that contributes to a new cultural market. Lazzarato argues that neoliberalism does not merely indicate a shift away from public sector funding and granting towards privatization, but a change in the mode of governing behaviour that emphasizes competition among individuals in a context of inequality that must be cultivated, regulated and maintained.[17] The name given to this type of cultural labour by post-operaists is immaterial labour. According to Michael Hardt and Antonio Negri, immaterial labour involves a contradictory "homogenization of labour processes" along with an increasing abstraction of labour, further estranging producers from what they produce.[18] As part of this contradictory process, they say, global capitalism creates a system of "direct communication between the production and consumption of commodities," inverting the relation between production planning and communication, and striving for "continual interactivity."[19] Moving in this direction of affective labour, often based on human contact and interaction, creating feelings of well-being and excitement, the cooperative powers of labour, they argue, "afford labour the possibility of valorizing itself."[20] In this, the cultural worker can hope to become a power not only "in itself" – i.e. the latest version of Canadian art as, precisely, *Canadian* art, as opposed to art from Canada or by Canadians – but "for itself." One of the fundamental difficulties within contemporary cultural theory is the adequate analysis of how this "for itself" is to be mediated.

There is, however, an alternative to the assumption that immaterial labour directly produces new communistic social relations and we can look for this in the cast-off of Hardt and Negri's theory: the Marxist theory of non-productive labour and the production of surplus value. Non-productive labour forms the background of the current interest in the productive capacities of the "creative class" and the rise of the service industry. To make things simple, we could say that an artist who makes work that is held to have intrinsic worth (aesthetic, cultural, social, political) is non-productive, whereas an artist who makes an art commodity that creates (economic) value for himself or a dealer is productive. In *Capital*, Marx gave as an example of these two possibilities the difference between a piano player and a piano maker. Unproductive labour overlaps significantly with the service sector of the economy, creating not only confusion for analysis but the realization on the part of economists that, in gross terms, something like sixty-five percent of the GDP and almost half of all Canadian and American employees provide services that *could* be characterized as unproductive.[21] Cultural production, inasmuch as it is supported by the public sector and contributes to public life, is not simply a measure of a good economy, adding to the diversification of human needs and enjoyment, but equally a site of competition and struggle, least of all because most cultural producers work for wages or are dependent on government grants. This is not because artists do not think about creating or finding audiences for their work, nor because the production of cultural goods is an inherently individual, creative act, but because art in a capitalist society has distinct ideological characteristics.

Contemporary culture is a result of modern specialization, reflexivity and an elaborate division of labour. Because of culture's function within the nexus of capitalist social relations, which measures value in terms of surplus, it becomes increasingly difficult to measure the non-productive value of creative labour. While non-productive labour can be associated with a host of functions that are useful to capitalist relations – mostly having to do with the maintenance of the institution of private property (accounting, advertising, management, banking, insurance, law, policing, security) – it can also be understood, in non-capitalist terms, as socially useful, contributing to social wealth, human development and well-being. The notion that labour in a capitalist economy is considered alienated labour does not imply that workers are unhappy, but rather that the value of productivity is only ever known "after the fact," once it has been measured in terms of profit.

The problem of productivity, the relation of productivity to the creation of surplus value, affects all forms of labour, including unproductive labour such as non-profit volunteer services, educational services, domestic labour or musical performance, for instance. Unproductive functions increase relative to the surplus produced by productive labour (production of tangible goods and services in the service of profit). The increase of non-productive labour is therefore an outcome of increased wealth, understood in terms of profit. It constitutes, however, and in capitalist terms, a destruction of wealth. Neoliberal policy therefore encourages the creation of social relations that maintain the class function of both productive and unproductive labour. We can therefore understand creative industries policies in relation to the current form of contemporary neoliberal governance, which seeks to maximize profits by making unproductive labour more "productive," minimizing the growth of unproductive labour through privatization and marketization at the same time that it continues to extract as much surplus as possible from

productive labour. Neoliberal sociologists, economists and politicians, therefore, understand the intrinsic worth of cultural products strictly in terms of their relation to profit.

One of the most perverse affirmations of this phenomenon, perverse because it does not seek to explain the link between the growth of non-productive labour and economic injustice, is Richard Florida's concept of the creative class, a theory of the occupations and lifestyle choices of creative and cognitive workers who work in large and mostly first world urban centres and whose expectations, he argues, should be the focus of local business and government.[22] The irony of Florida's research is that by economic definition, most artists would not qualify for inclusion in his creative class category. According to Florida, the creative sector, representing thirty percent of the workforce and distinguished from services and manufacturing, includes those employed in fields like science, engineering, architecture, design, arts, music, entertainment, law, business, finance, health care and related fields, especially those that can be linked to education and technological innovation. Members of the creative class, he states, earn an annual average above $55,000US. In contrast, the service class that the creative economy relies upon, composed of janitors, housecleaners, food-service workers, nurses and clerks, on average receive less than $22,000US in wages per year. Based on earnings, a good many members of the creative sector can therefore be thought to be part of the broader service sector. This also applies inasmuch as they are involved in service relations, where values are consumed at the point they are produced.

The subtlety of Florida's idea of a creative economy, which he associates with the new conditions of global economic competitiveness, is its collapse of the notion of social class – once visible in the institutional divide between trade schools and universities, intellectual and manual labour – and the quality of "creativity," an innate capacity for innovation that he links with a quasi-Darwinian notion of adaptation.[23] The idea of adaptation not only structures his model of individual creativity, but applies to the whole of his research. It represents the ability of cities, regions and nations to stimulate economic growth by attracting and retaining creative talent, and thus, surviving in the economy of the future. Florida's use of the concept of creativity works nominally, disappearing behind a plethora of statistics that are used to buttress his political argument in favour of neoliberalism with a human (bohemian-gay) face. The politics of adaptation, in which the interests of the creative class are divided and mystified by the quest for individual status and economic success, returns, however, as political parties negotiate the future of the creative class in terms of tax breaks for the middle class and for corporations, debt reduction, privatization of services and economic growth, on the one hand, and the protection of jobs through government programs and social investment on the other.

It should be said that Florida is hardly the only scholar promoting the virtues of creative innovation. He is perhaps one of the more progressive-seeming speakers in the strange world that combines motivational psychology with public policy. This work is consistent with the neoconservative "attack on the professions" which blames hierarchies in fields of knowledge as barriers to economic stimulation. Beginning in the late 1970s, and as part of the reaction of New Right governments to welfarism, public institutions were brutally restructured, the argument went, so they could "survive" economically in the marketplace. Increasing the power of centralized authority, neoliberal governments also oversaw a shift from manufacturing (that is, in the developed West, where labour standards increase production costs) to a service economy, creating an unstable employment structure with growth in the consumption of "immaterial" and leisure services. As a result, a flexible, skilled and educated workforce has become a permanent feature of the new service economy. Neoliberal thinkers like Florida, Charles Leadbeater, Daniel Pink and Sir Ken Robinson by and large disguise the politics of their neoliberal policy research with humanistic language of disinterested pleasure and free inquiry, arguably the conditions that would produce the next Yo-Yo Ma or Bill Gates.

The kinds of cultural production that are encouraged by recourse to concepts like creative class and creative cities are nefarious if not undemocratic. One example of this is the recent creation of The Canada Prize for the Arts and Creativity by two Toronto businessmen, which was bankrolled by more than $35M in provincial and federal tax dollars. The Prize, like the Luminato Festival that was created by these same individuals, creates a corporate friendly environment for large-scale spectacles that are out of the reach of most Canadian artists. It siphons funding from the progressive arts sector and transforms it into an instrument of marketing. It creates precarious work opportunities rather than formal training and it leaves out in the cold those professionally trained artists who are increasingly dependent on the grants made available by university degree programs to remain independent of economic motivation.

The popularity of Florida's work within the Canadian bureaucratic class provides an important indication that a creative industry model like the one established in the U.K. under New Labour and through the creation of the Department for Culture, Media and Sport has already been adopted by Canadian politicians and policy makers. According to Angela McRobbie, idealist concepts like creativity, talent and success are popular with today's policy makers because they dispense with the untidy business of critical sociology. Instead, creativity, channeled in the direction of entrepreneurial activity and freelance work, provides a framework for the model individual of the new economy, an independent businessperson who can free themselves from social welfare support and who can be left to their own devices in terms of job creation.[24] Placing emphasis on the creative entrepreneur also allows politicians to shift attention away from big corporations, where most job losses occur. This model of the highly educated and resourceful artist is also useful to today's governments despite the fact that job creation by and large takes place elsewhere, in particular, in the software industries and security sector. It completely ignores the job insecurity, unemployment and bankruptcies that characterize the working conditions of the large mass of excluded practices that exist in the shadows of the institutionalized art world.

Cultural Resistance Today

A cultural politics worthy of the name should be able to offer a political analysis of creative labour. Such an analysis, directed against the exploitative expropriation of labour runs up against neoliberal policies that seek to regulate creative labour through capital investment in creative industries. According to Aras Ozgun, the business and government architects of the creative industries discourse recognize that the individuals, collectives and small businesses that constitute the creative class show a high degree of creative innovation, an ability to assess trends, a high level of education, skill in the area of digital technologies and links to both the private and public sectors. Their goal, however, is to change the small business structure and lack of marketing orientation of creative work and orient production towards economic growth and export. One major problem with this shift towards industrial scale production is the introduction of exploitative practices, market regulation and the forceful disciplining of labour.[25]

Creative industries policies therefore fall in line with neoliberal politics and its goal of capitalization through the imposition of labour discipline. The maintenance of unemployment, low wages, competition for jobs, de-unionization, outsourcing, work speed-up and innovation, the combination of flexibilization and neo-Taylorization in management, and capital investment in the industrialization of culture, it is hoped, will contribute to the management of falling rates of profit. While some welcomed the news that the 2009 federal budget included $60M for arts infrastructure (and millions more for heritage, tourism, television, broadcasting, sports, parks and the international cruise ship industry), we should keep in mind that investment in new museums, libraries, cultural centers, production facilities, studios and educational programs is designed to increase the rate of surplus value. It does not in any way take into consideration the fundamental basis of the creative industries: namely, the expropriation of labour.

How then could we link the surplus value that the creative industries are designed to generate with artistic practice? One would need to provide some insight into the ideological workings of culture that are at the heart of today's construction of creativity as a motor of economic growth. What artists produce under capitalist relations of production are commodities and consumer services. Because of this, it becomes increasingly difficult for artists to know themselves as producers.[26] Whereas the free creation of culture requires that we assume our own enjoyment of activity without further mediation, capitalist relations construe the artist as the consumer of his or her own activity. The commodity is the means by which I, the artist, am included my own production; it is that which bears witness to my social existence, the Thing whose "metaphysical subtlety" lies precisely in my social interactions with others but which nevertheless leads me to believe in its magical powers.

The point here is that the subject is not the absolute correlate of the commodity. In the context of the depoliticization of cultural production, the first task of the artist is to debunk the symbolic innocence of a global culture industry and to reassert the state of alienation. Such an act reveals the close connection between the class of arts managers and policy makers with the creative class and its reserve army of surplus labour. An example of this can be noticed in the recent mobilization of a number of European unions against the Lisbon strategy in higher education, a plan to "modernize" the public educational system in the direction of knowledge markets. The call to mobilize is directed against the marketization of scientific and educational activities, against the generalized competition of people and territories, and for an emancipatory and democratic public service of higher education and research.

Today's talk of the creative class, the creative industries and the artist as a business person construes the cultural worker as an exception – according to Slavoj Žižek, "an element which, although part of the system, does not have a proper place within it" and cannot be accounted for in its terms.[27] Perhaps one indication of this, provided by Richard Hardacre, is the fact that the Harper Conservatives can try to convince the electorate that the creative industries receive handouts, whereas the automotive and other industries receive investments. But this is only half the story. What happens when the arts begin to receive investments like the manufacturing sector and banks? What happens, as Žižek asks, when the system no longer excludes this "part with no part," but directly posits it as a driving force? This is not only the question of our day but also the basis for a radical approach to cultural production.

Postscript

In October of 2009 Stephen Harper attended a fundraising event for the National Youth and Education Trust at the National Arts Centre in Ottawa. Once again the media celebrated Harper's piano playing as he sang the Beatles song *With a Little Help from My Friends* to the accompaniment of the famous cellist Yo-Yo Ma. The audience, along with members of the opposition, gave him a standing ovation, almost as though they were surprised that a person with so little charisma could show signs of life. Harper's charity of course goes hand in hand with his government's privatization agenda. Only a few months later, Harper prorogued parliament for a period of three months. This was the second time his government did this in less than two years. The first time, a coalition of opposition parties would have ousted him from office had it not been for the Liberal Party's cowering to pressure from the big banks. The question that becomes pertinent here is under what conditions does cultural productivity manage to win popular approbation. There is no sign of cultural integrity or relevance in Harper's performance, only a clearing of the stage for the exchange of money.

Harper's next foray into populist entertainment was in the lead-up to the 2011 federal election. Shortly after the election was announced in March the Conservative Party of Canada put out a mean-spirited advertisement that stated that opposition parties were soft on immigration policy, a fact that ignores the immense wealth and potential that this North American territory holds for millions of immigrants and refugees that would like to make their home in Canada. The ad depicted the MV Sun Sea, a ship that brought 491 Tamil refugees to the shores of British Columbia in August 2010, and accused the refugees of criminally abusing the generosity of Canadians. Almost as if to make up for a bad start to his election campaign, Stephen Harper arranged for him and his spouse to meet with Maria Aragon, a ten-year old Filipino-Canadian whose cover of Lady Gaga's "Born This Way" became something of a sensation on YouTube. In early April, a YouTube video was posted of Harper accompanying Aragon on the piano and singing with her John Lennon's "Imagine." According to Stefan Christoff, the lyrics of John Lennon's popular song are the exact opposite of Harper's "nationalist, war-driven foreign policy."[28]

Given that the Harper government's single solution to everything is to privatize, this follow-up to his 2009 performance of "With a Little Help From My Friends" merely indicated that his plan for culture had not changed since the previous election. The content and social value of a song like "Imagine," which gives it more than just a certain popularity, has apparently no bearing on its manipulative appropriation. One might think so if Yoko Ono, the widow of John Lennon and trustee of Lenono Music, had not requested that YouTube remove the video for copyright reasons.[29] The fact that Lenono Music has not requested that thousands of other covers be removed, including one rendered by Bill Clinton, is a clear indication of a thumbs down for Harper's anti-democratic free market politics. All things considered, Harper's singing of "Imagine" fell flat with anyone who knows what John and Yoko stood for. The misappropriation didn't work. No sooner had the Harper government been re-elected with a minority vote, Brigette DePape, a parliamentary page, interrupted Harper's inaugural throne speech by occupying the floor of the Senate and pulling out a red stop sign with the words Stop Harper. DePape told reporters that she wished there would come a Canadian version of the Arab Spring. That fall, on October 15, cities across Canada joined the #Occupy Wall Street movement and in the spring of 2012 Québec students led a remarkable and victorious struggle against austerity that today links the symbol of the red square to the Strike Debt campaign in the U.S. and to worldwide "Global Noise" anti-austerity protests. These are two occasions in which new forms of collective cultural production are enacted that go beyond the cash nexus and refuse the biocapitalist engineering of life.

Protesting Degree Zero: On Black Bloc Tactics, Culture and Building the Movement

Among some of the images of good citizenship generated by the mainstream media following the demonstrations against the meeting of G8 and G20 leaders in Toronto from June 25 to 27, 2010, two particular cases come to mind.[1] The first, broadcast repeatedly on the morning of June 27 by the local Toronto television news station *CP24*, was an interview with a private security expert who had spotted two demonstrators emerge from an underground sewer. The middle-aged man described them as though they were unwanted vermin that he took pleasure in rooting out.[2] Although there was not much to this story, it aired repeatedly like a mantra for the weekend. A second similar image was of a local banker on his time off, tackling a Black Bloc demonstrator as he fled from a Bell mobile phone retailer with a stolen package of some sort in his hands. Given a prominent photo spread by the *National Post*, the man could also be seen in action on YouTube taking a BlackBerry package out of the scrambling protester's hands and exclaiming "Don't steal."[3] The attitudes of these two men were far from what we might expect from people who are violently opposed to anarchistic rioting or who are hardcore right-wingers. Instead, their opposition to the movement seemed rather like the attitude of many of the demonstrators themselves during the protests: somewhat bemused and enthused by the excitement generated by the conflict. If the confrontation of police and demonstrators reflects the opposition of the forces of social justice versus those of obscene exploitation, state power and social inequality, then perhaps the face-off between merry-making protesters and bemused mainstream onlookers gives an indication of the more subtle and pervasive structures of ideology that structure the social space as a whole.

In his book on violence, Slavoj Žižek suggests that there are three kinds of violence: subjective acting out, the symbolic violence embodied in language and social norms, and the systemic violence that comes about as a result of the smooth functioning of economic and political systems.[4] His argument is that subjective and systemic violence cannot be perceived from the same standpoint, and so, to extrapolate, what in some ways occurs in protest situations is an effort to subjectively embody or instantiate the background "zero degree," the normal state of things that is sustained by objective violence. What counts as violence, what enters the space of our ideological consciousness and what is able to affect social change, depends upon ideologico-political considerations. The problem of violence, Žižek argues, is that it is almost impossible to confront directly because it eludes symbolic mediation. The left-liberal humanitarian call to stop this objective, systemic violence, he further suggests, has an anti-theoretical edge, and we find a similar anti-theoreticism in the presuppositions of non-mediation and non-representativity that colour anarchist thought. The pseudo-urgency of radical calls to action, Žižek argues, are premised on a notion of immediacy that is a symptomatic aspect of the liberal focus on subjective violence.

This essay considers the use of Black Bloc tactics at anti-capitalist demonstrations with a particular focus on the 2010 Toronto protest marches. My thesis is that the calculated use of "violence," usually the smashing of windows of retail chain stores, can be cautiously approached through an aesthetic appreciation of political action – politics interpreted through the lens of culture. I relate Black Bloc tactics to three works of contemporary art that examine contemporary conflicts in terms of training and role-playing. While anarchist politics typically refuse the logic of representation, mediation could be said to return in the symbolic performance of conflict. The fact that capital feeds on subjective violence, and the fact that systemic violence cannot be attributed to individuals, as Žižek argues, allows us to perceive both the merits of anarchist practice and some of its theoretical limitations. On the one hand, due to the basic anarchist principle of non-hierarchy, Black Blocers refuse to do harm to individuals during demonstrations. In fact, most anarchists do not consider the destruction of things to be acts of violence. At the same time, anarchist politics are typically libertarian, asserting not so much class conflict as the autonomy of each and every one of us, either bypassing the socially mediated nature of subjectivity in capitalist society or fetishizing it through a politics of anti-racism, anti-patriarchy, anti-normativity, etc. Through Black Bloc actions, I argue in this paper, ideology reappears in the anarchist politics of unmediated transparency as a condition for the explosion of subjective violence.

Wild in the Streets

The following provides a cursory look at anti-summit organizing in the days leading up to and following the G8 and G20 summits in Huntsville and Toronto.[5] I rely for the most part on articles published online on the *rabble.ca* website, a progressive left media source that is supported by individual subscribers, foundations and labour unions. In particular, the journalist Krystalline Kraus maintained a "G8/G20 Communique" with the heading: "This blog is about the anti-G8/G20 lead up events and protests in June 2010. She believes in Diversity of Tactics because that's how the natural world works. Hooray for Diversity!" I myself participated in the demonstrations on June 25 and 26 and traveled to Toronto in the company of some 500 Montrealers who took buses organized by the CLAC, the *Convergence des luttes anti-capitalistes*/Convergence of anti-capitalist struggles.

In the days leading up to the events, Kraus provided reports on what to do if police come knocking at your door, asking questions about your political activities. Since the Fall of 2009, the Royal Canadian Mounted Police (RCMP) and the Canadian Security and Intelligence Service (CSIS) had been paying visits to social justice organizers and activists in order to create divisions between activists, to catalog psychological profiles, to plant misinformation and to intimidate people more generally. A People's Commission Network was established before June by lawyers who gave the recommendation to not talk to police, from then until the weekend of the 26th, when 10,000 police and 5,000 private security personnel would be patrolling the downtown area. A temporary jail was prepared by the police in an old movie studio just five kilometres away from the where the summit was to take place. A security perimeter with a three kilometre long and three metre high fence was built around the summit site and was to be guarded by the Integrated Security Unit, comprised of the RCMP, the Ontario Provincial Police, the Toronto Police Service, the Canadian Armed Forces, and the Peel Regional Police. Some seventy-seven CCTV cameras had been added to the downtown area and costs for security were reported to have added up to one billion dollars. LRAD sound cannons and water cannons had been purchased as well as other crowd dispersal weapons. The police would not rule out the use of agents provocateurs and in fact admitted that they would use crowd infiltrators at the G20 summit to take the pulse of the crowd. Richard Fadden, director of CSIS, told the CBC that terrorist attacks were unlikely and that the real threat would come from "anarchist groups" and "multi-issue extremists" who seek media attention.

In the days leading up to the protests, various social movement groups organized events to voice their issues: global justice groups, peace activists, environment and climate change activists (with a People's Assembly on Climate), human rights activists, civil liberties organizers, first nations representatives, women's groups (responding to abortion issues in particular) and queer activists (focusing on the Toronto pride parade and the pro-Palestine issue in particular as well as AIDS activism). Kraus lamented in her June 4 communiqué that not enough had been done to meet the Toronto Community Mobilization

Network's "Accessibility Guidelines" and to include persons with disabilities in meetings.

On June 21 a taste of possible police repression made it into the news as three individuals were charged by Ottawa police for firebombing a branch of the Royal Bank of Canada. The charges of "domestic terrorism" against the three relatively unknown and self-described anarchists cast a chill on activists who almost unanimously dismissed the action as irresponsible. This event prompted a shift in reporting away from the various social movement issues to the business of protesting. Kraus subsequently gave her first report on Black Bloc tactics:

> The Black Bloc: I say "might" because that person might just be anti-social but you should note that dressing in all black demarks a member of the Black Bloc or anarchist movement. And yes, I've heard the scary claims and hysteria about how the Black Bloc eats babies but I've also personally seen members of the Black Bloc go out of their way to help other activists in trouble by providing cover and tactical know-how since they are usually well trained, committed and know what to do at a demo.[6]

On June 25, the day of a peaceful march organized by the Toronto Community Mobilization Network (an ad-hoc group of activist organizers), David Coles, President of the Communications, Energy and Paperworks Union (CEP), provided the usual labour union position on anarchist direct action, denouncing in advance any possible use of violence by demonstrators. With this, Coles indicated that protesters should not be blamed by public opinion for the exorbitant cost of security since social democrats at least condemn such uses of violence. As it turned out, and as expected, the first demonstration by about 5000 protesters was peaceful, with marchers returning to Allan Gardens Park and making plans for the evening.

On Saturday June 26, the march from Queen's Park (the provincial parliament building) towards the downtown and back was divided in advance into two tactical sections: the People First March (the so-called "green zone" march overseen by labour unions and NGOs) and the Get Off the Fence March (the so-called "red zone" in which demonstrators would seek to make it to the fence in acts of both civil disobedience and direct action involving Black Bloc tactics). In anticipation of the latter, some twenty or so activists and organizers had been arrested overnight. The well-known feminist activist Judy Rebick advocated for the green Labour/NGO/Peace March while at the same time denouncing the massive police presence designed to vilify those who stand for justice. The demonstration, as things unfolded, marched West on Queen Street and turned Northward up Spadina back towards Queen's Park. At this point, red zone demonstrators held back and a Black Bloc was formed that traveled East on Queen and North on Yonge. Whether actual protesters or agents provocateurs, they destroyed a number of police vehicles, a CBC van, and dozens of chain store windows. Such actions were anticipated. For instance, the Southern Ontario Anarchist Resistance declared in the days preceding: "This action will be militant and confrontational, seeking to humiliate the security apparatus and make Toronto's elites regret letting the dang G20 in here." As the smashing took place, police practically ignored the destruction, allowing it to happen. Instead, the police turned on demonstrators who had assembled at Queen's Park and began a wave of brutal arrests that lasted into the night, adding up over the weekend to approximately one thousand arrests.

In the evening of June 26, the morning of the 27th and for days after that, the media was awash with images and descriptions of Black Bloc demonstrators. While Toronto Police Chief Bill Blair correctly informed the media public that the Black Bloc was not a group but a tactic, Toronto Mayor David Miller accused Blocers of not being legitimate protesters and being mere criminals. A spokesperson for the Prime Minister described them as thugs that do not represent the Canadian way of life. In contrast, a report in the *Toronto Star* provided this more glamorous account:

> As suddenly as they burst onto the streets, they vanished into the crowd. The men and women, clad in black clothes, their faces obscured with bandanas, ski goggles and gas masks, had spent the last hour storming through city streets, hurling rocks and debris through the windows of banks and big-chain stores.[7]

The reporter goes on to explain the Black Bloc tactic, the use of black clothes to hide individual identities, and the causes its participants support. On Sunday, residents of Toronto assessed the damage and tourists walked around like in a dream, directed to and fro by police officers. Everyone was a possible suspect.

Activists like Rebick were pressed in the days following the demonstrations to emphasize that the 25,000 protesters had been "overwhelmingly peaceful" and that labour organizers had tried in vain to keep the march from getting rowdy. She denounced the police for letting "the mob" in black clothes destory banks and trash Yonge Street:

> Like David [Coles] I believe the cops could have arrested the Black Bloc right at the beginning of the action but they abandoned their police cars and allowed them to burn, not even calling the fire department until the media had lots of time to photograph them. They had a water cannon but they didn't even use a fire extinguisher. Why?[8]

Rebick and noted journalist Naomi Klein accused the police of playing politics.[9] In her report Rebick added:

I disagree with torching police cars and breaking windows and I have been debating these tactics for decades with people who think they accomplish something. But the bigger question here is why the police let it happen and make no mistake the police did let it happen. Why did the police let the city get out of control? And they did let it get out of control. The police knew exactly what would happen and how. (...) It was a perfect storm. A massive police presence [that was] primed for "dangerous anarchists" after a week of peaceful protests. No more than one hundred, probably fewer young men who think violent confrontations with the police will create a radicalization and expose the violence of the state.[10]

This article garnered many comments, some of them mentioning the fact that women also participated in the Bloc. One young woman could be seen on YouTube twirling an umbrella so that cameras could not capture the image of her mates. Another comment stated that it was ironic that the "left" had been reduced to complaining about the lack of policing.

Fred Wilson, Assistant to the President of the CEP and member of the Board of Directors of the Council of Canadians, asserted that lapdog reporters first responded to police chiefs and conservative ministers without consulting with the organizers of the march, namely, the Canadian Labour Congress, the Council of Canadians, Greenpeace, Oxfam and the Canadian Federation of Students. He stated:

I don't buy for a moment the argument that media will always take the most dramatic image and that the lack of focus on what actually happened is the fault of a few violent anarchists who discredited the many. Nonsense. A far more compelling image was the sight of many hundreds of young Greenpeace members wearing green hardhats with labels calling for good green jobs. It was a truly stunning image, more interesting than the one we saw over an over again of a lone person smashing a window. No, this is about a hierarchy of images. Choices are made.[11]

Wilson makes the interesting claim that vandalism crosses a line that labour and social movements should deal with but the actual "dealing with" is usually limited to denunciations, comparing Black Blocers, as Wilson did, to sports fans that maraud through streets after a sports series victory. Wilson adds that trade unionists had come to Toronto from fifty different countries to debate the crisis of economic sustainability and that none of this was reported in the news media. The fact that the largest demonstration since the Québec City Free Trade Area of the Americas actions in 2001 *could* be reduced to Black Bloc violence, however, should indeed be reason to deal with it in such a way as to overcome the usual split between support for diversity of tactics and social democratic denunciations. I would add, however, and before doing so, that the security costs for the Pittsburgh and London summits had been closer to $100 million than $1 billion. The then French President, Nicolas Sarkozy, took the opportunity to upstage the Canadian Prime Minister, Stephen Harper, saying that he could do as well as the U.S. in such matters.

As the days passed, the commentary turned somewhat paranoid. According to a senior editor at *rabble*, Murray Dobbin, the decision to allow the Black Bloc to do its destructive reactionary work was part of a strategic operation to entrench conservative politics. In this, he argued, the Black Blocers should have to answer for themselves. Activists should perhaps try to stop them, he wrote: "They are the enemies of social change – we should treat all of them as *agents provocateurs* and plan to deal with them accordingly."[12] Dobbin here reverses the usual argument that since the Black Bloc is likely comprised of undercover police, and there are no limits to police repression, we should simply strategically accept the diversity of tactics so as to not exclude comrades and break ranks. Dobbin says instead that by stopping Blocers we might catch more police in the act of deceiving the public. One cannot build a radical movement, however, by catching police but rather by outnumbering them, and hopefully, eventually, by winning them over to our side – making them in name and in fact "our cops."[13] To conclude, our erstwhile dispatcher, Krystalline Kraus, reported that as of July 3, polls indicated that the vast majority of Canadians believed that police violence against G20 protesters was justified, that the demonstrations were shameful, disgusting and maddening. The only thing we can know for sure is that a majority of Torontonians had watched the protests closely through the mediation of television news.[14]

Twice Around the Bloc

One of the issues that is not addressed by social movement denunciations of Black Bloc tactics is the specific political philosophy that animates anarchist politics. Social democratic unions misinform the public and their own members when they ignore the fact that most anarchists who attack summit meetings are producing a direct instantiation of their politics, without the political mediation of elected state officials. Against the Canadian Union of Public Employees (CUPE) representative who stated that Black Bloc demonstrators felt powerless to "change the direction of their elected leaders," a minimum of political sophistication requires that we recognize the anti-statist politics of most anarchists. In contrast to civil disobedience, which, as David Graeber explains, is designed to sway public opinion, direct action, such as Black Bloc property destruction, is based on the principles of non-representative self-organization and voluntary association. Black Bloc tactics are opposed to coercive authority and are undertaken with the knowledge that collective action can be met with hostile intervention on the part of state police.[15]

In a useful summary of what to say or do about Black Bloc tactics, Graeber considers whether it is legitimate to condemn such principled acts of violence. What strikes many of us in the movement is the serial nature of the media commentary on broken windows at anti-capitalist protests. As Graeber puts it:

> Some will argue that confrontational tactics or property destruction only make activists look bad in the eyes of the public. Others will argue the corporate media wouldn't make us look good whatever we do. Some will argue that if you smash a Starbucks window, that will be the only story on the news, effectively freezing out any consideration of issues; others will reply that if there's no property destruction, there won't be any story at all. Some will claim confrontational tactics deprive activists of the moral high ground; others will accuse those people of being elitist, and insist that the violence of the system is so overwhelming that unless one creates some sort of peace police to physically threaten anyone who spray paints or breaks a window, some will probably do so, and if so, coordinating with the militants rather than isolating them is much safer for all concerned. In the end, it almost always invariably ends up with the same resolution: that as long as no one is actually attacking another human being, the important thing is to maintain solidarity.[16]

Graeber adds that the last thing anyone wants is for pacifists to have to resort to physically attacking their comrades, as happened in Seattle.

The 1999 anti-globalization protest in Seattle is an important event in the spread of Black Bloc tactics in North America. It should be said that there are many "bloc" formations, representing different attitudes and outlooks, including the Silver and Pink Bloc, Green Bloc, Critical Mass Bike Bloc, White Bloc (i.e. Tute Bianche and Ya Basta!), Clown Bloc, Book Bloc, Medieval

Bloc, Naked Bloc, Raging Grannies, Radical Cheerleaders and Samba Blocs, to name a few, and to not forget the terrifying Zombie Bloc that I witnessed at the Toronto G20. The Black Bloc is therefore only one type of collective action and there is nothing that prevents someone from participating in more than one form of Bloc activity. The idea of a bloc is to provide security for participants as it carries out an action in the midst of a demonstration. It represents the convergence of many affinity groups and is unlike traditional militant formations in terms of its small scale, which allows actors to negotiate amongst themselves the course of action. Given that Black Blocers will often carry out the destruction of symbols of corporate and state violence, the black clothing and masks that they wear allows them to avoid police identification. By shedding their dark clothes after an action, they can disappear into the crowd of demonstrators and onlookers.

According to social scientist François Dupuis-Déri, the Black Bloc tactic originated with "autonomous" squatters in Germany in the 1980s.[17] Neither inherently anarchist, nor associated with mainstream left labour organizations, autonomous groups spread throughout Germany to Holland and Denmark, refusing rent payments, organizing university occupations and squats, and fighting neo-Nazi skinheads. When the city of Berlin decided to crack down on squatters, the police named them "schwarzer Bloc" for the black clothing that they wore. The Black Bloc tactic was used on several occasions in Europe throughout the 1980s and is considered an effective tactic that is useful in the contestation of state power.[18] It was used in 1991 in the U.S. to protest the war against Iraq, to protest Columbus Day, and again in April of 1999, to protest the emprisonment of Mumia Abu-Jamal. Largely owing to the notoriety of the Seattle protests against the World Trade Organization, it was used throughout the 2000s in numerous anti-summit and anti-globalization demonstrations.

In the aftermath of Seattle, Michael Albert wrote a now popular anti-Black Bloc tract called "On Trashing and Movement Building."[19] In this text, Albert begins with the assertion that "as far as violence is concerned," the greatest share of blame and condemnation should be reserved for the state and global capitalist forces. While window smashing fights injustice, he claims, oligarchic forces contribute to it. The issue of tactics within social movements, however, of property damage and civil disobedience, nevertheless requires some kind of mediation since, he argues, such tactics endanger people, dilute the message of the activists, and provide a pretext for police to provoke hostilities. For Albert, breaking windows goes against most protesters' norms and can turn adventurist. Consequently, there can be no unyielding principle of direct action since what is warranted in any given situation is variable. Here, theory and practice seem to confront one another without Albert providing an adequate theory of practice. Activists of the trashing mindset, he asserts, don't care to calculate the social outcomes of their actions, but value them in themselves. The only issue then, he says, is what target to hit. The difficulty, as he sees it, is that violent tactics impose an unfair burden on the rest of the demonstrators and usurp those who show a supportive mix of militant creativity and organizational intelligence. He writes:

> Changing society isn't a matter of breaking windows, it is a process of developing consciousness and vehicles of organization and movement, and of then applying these to win gains that benefit deserving constituencies and create conditions for still further victories, leading to permanent institutional change.

Trashing, he concludes, can have no positive effects since it does not win visibility or enlarge democracy but causes onlookers to feel that dissent in general is aberrant. Albert concludes that the emotional turmoil of anticipation, rage and paranoia are useless as agents of change.

As defenders of anti-capitalist anarchist politics, Graeber and Dupuis-Déri argue for a deeper appreciation of the small-scale, decentred and autonomous organizing of anarchist cells. Moreover, the anarchist philosophy of anti-hierarchy allows us to perceive Black Blocers as an important political force rather than as juvenile delinquents. One indication of the strength of Black Bloc tactics, according to Dupuis-Déri, is the fact that since Seattle and the successful cancellation of the WTO meetings, global capitalist police forces have resorted to systematic arrests, lies and humiliation directed against the global justice movement. The routine of infiltrations and arrests sends a clear message for those who want to hear it that many are actively opposing state violence. To not know what all the fuss is about, he says, is to really not want to know much about anything.[20] In this the Bloc is also directed at the social movement itself and those within it – most notably social democratic labour unions and non-governmental organizations – who are not prepared to consider a radical critique of the economic and political system.[21] Black Blocers therefore actively invite and may very well scoff at the criticism of reformists. The crisis they wish to point to is the crisis of representative democracy.

Within the anarchist movement there is a will to a different form of political participation that is informed by the Paris Commune, utopian socialism, workers' councils and Soviets, the May '68 student movement and the new social movements of feminists, ecologists and queer collectives. Respect for the diversity of tactics, the refusal to tell someone else that violence, in any given form, is unwarranted and prohibited, derives from the granting of respect and autonomy to all of those involved. Political elites, in contrast, encourage social democrats to discipline those among the protesters who are likely to cause trouble, leading to a routine, Dupuis-Déri says, wherein union elites, official political elites and the police make demands and negotiate permits that allow protest organizers to discipline their troops so that the police do not have to intervene.[22] In contrast, Black Blocers do not seek to include representatives at meetings or become media spokespeople, but rather look to local participation where deliberative politics are possible. For Graeber, the recent thrust of anarchist organizing is largely an outcome of the ecology movement of the 1970s and principles of organizing that were developed in Quaker communities. The movement has of course a broader history, however, from early twentieth-century anarchism and the Wobblies to the New Left and the Zapatistas. Aside from the sometimes offensive hygiene, the hippie-punk style and the vegetarian diet (some of it gleaned from dumpsters!), Graeber lists a number of features that can be said to describe both anarchists and Black Blocers: acting for oneself without the mediation of authorities, a readiness to fight and to take power for oneself, self-reliance, mutual aid, voluntary association, collectivity and courage. The goal of anarchist politics is to create change from the ground up, from small temporary communities to permanent, free societies.

Graeber makes the usual claim that while anarchists and Marxists have a potential complementarity (despite bitter and violent disagreements), anarchism is not an ideology, nor a theory of history. Typically, anarchists decry class inequality but do not provide a class analysis. Moreover, anarchists tend to dispense with ideology critique, positing an unmediated relation between the means of production and the social relations of production, as witnessed in the work of Gilles Deleuze and Félix Guattari and in the autonomous Marxist line of theorizing. Contemporary anarchism has to a large extent become a progressive politics that suits the lifestyle concerns of North Americans' "classless" view of themselves and is compatible with the identity politics of feminists, queers and racial minorities. The recent wave of interest in anarchism thus has two main historical causes: the resurgence of anti-capitalist politics since the 1990s, on the one hand, and postmodern anti-foundationalism on the other. The latter, with its academic post-structuralism, seeks to dispense with, deconstruct, and reject every Master-Signifier, allowing for no rules, no social norms, no binding decisions, and facilitating the commodification of everything. On this issue, I am in agreement with Žižek who argues that leftists need to rethink tactical alliances and compromises with liberals who generate politics around culture wars.[23]

Graeber addresses this question of culture wars and identity politics versus political orthodoxy through an examination of Murray Bookchin's essay on "social anarchism versus lifestyle anarchism," which he reads as an attempt to keep artists and bohemians distinct from revolutionaries. Graeber argues that such an attempt is futile since people have the need to rebel against alienation as well as oppression.[24] Interestingly, he expresses the rebellion against alienation in terms of culture and creativity, alluding to the DIY ethos of punks, the craftsperson orientation of hippie culture, and forms of lifestyling that balance the two kinds of revolt. In the section on "Representation" in his book *Direct Action*, Graeber argues that anarchists are typically less interested in post-68 thought, in Deleuze, Foucault and Baudrillard, than in the militant 60s writings of thinkers like Frantz Fanon, Guy Debord and Raoul Vaneigem. The fascination with power/knowledge in academia began in the 70s and 80s. Consequently, academics found themselves increasingly isolated from social movements as they abdicated critique in favour of theory.

Debord and the Situationists, in contrast to postmodernists, advocated revolutionary struggle and, in keeping with the work of Henri Lefebvre, the critique of everyday life (as opposed to its celebration). In his *Revolution of Everyday Life*, Vaneigem excoriated left liberals:

> Look at peace marchers, aside from an active minority of radicals, most of them are nothing but penitents trying to exorcise their desire to disappear with all the rest of humanity. They would deny it, of course, but their miserable faces give them away. The only real joy is revolutionary.[25]

Vaneigem opposed the pleasure of subversion and contempt for the future to the general state of survival and the consolations of consumerism. He sought in particular to rescue subjectivity through the pleasure of destruction: "Better to die on our feet than live on our knees."[26] He opposed issue politics in particular, with its piecemeal demands and its reformist acceptance of successive sacrifices. Against socialist ennui, he advocated a propaganda of the deed. The despairing tactics of the anarchist terrorist should be altered into modern strategy and come to resemble the childishness of teenage gangs who aspire to poetry by wanting more, by wanting to understand revolutionary consciousness. Tactics, he surmised, "are the polemical stage of play. They provide the necessary continuity between poetry *in statu nascendi* (play) and the organisation of spontaneity (poetry). Essentially technical in nature, they prevent spontaneity burning itself out in the general confusion."[27] The goal of the Situationist International, he concluded after pages that link play with discipline and coherence, is to "kindle the fire of working-class guerilla warfare."[28] While many of Graeber's colleagues, a "post-student" core of activists as he calls them, have in some ways lost the thread of revolutionary thought, he is not far from the truth when he argues that Black Blocers appear as the latest avatar of the artistic/revolutionary tradition that stretches back to the Dadaists and the Situationists, a tradition that "plays off the contradictions of capitalism by turning its own destructive, leveling forces against it."[29] It is on this Saint-Simonian ideal of the artist as political leader that I turn to some considerations of contemporary art that explores protest space, police tactics and role-playing in contemporary societies of control.

Aesthetics, Politics, History

In June of 1984 the National Union of Mineworkers organized a mass picket of 6000 union members from across the U.K. Their grievance was against the British Steel coking plant in Orgreave, South Yorkshire, which was allowing scab labour to maintain production levels higher than the union considered sustainable. The NUM, wishing to prevent pit closures and save working communities, saw itself confronting not only one employer, but also the government of Margaret Thatcher, which was working to break union power and impose market forces. The "Battle of Orgreave," which took place on June 18, had been preceded by bitter strikes in Toxteth and Brixton. On this occasion, the NUM tried to blockade the Orgreave plant and force a temporary closure. The police, making use of colonial riot tactics, infiltrator moles, shields, foot soldiers, attack dogs and cavalry, deployed some 8000 troops from ten countries. While the battle lasted for up to one year, the events of June 18 are remembered for the scale of the conflict. Ninety-three arrests were made, fifty-one pickets and seventy-two police were injured, and ninety-five pickets

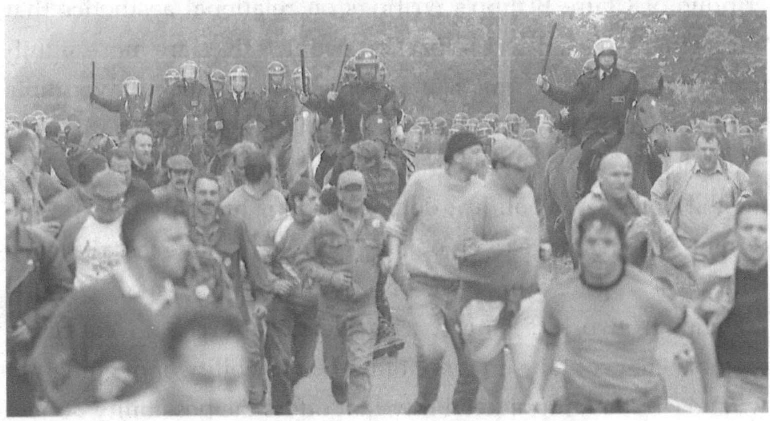

Jeremy Deller, *The Battle of Orgreave*, 2001. Photos Martin Jenkinson. Courtesy of Artangel.

were charged with riot and unlawful assembly. In 1987 lawsuits were brought against the police, leading in 1991 to the police having to pay half of one million pounds in damages.

In 2001, the artist Jeremy Deller was awarded a large commission by the art agency Artangel Media to organize a reenactment of the miners' strike. Deller hired Howard Giles, a leading battle re-creator, to research court testimonies, oral accounts and newspaper reports and to prepare a production of the re-enactment through the Historical Films Services. Giles worked with filmmaker Mike Figgis to direct 800 people, including 200 local people in Orgreave, some of them ex-miners and some of them former policemen. The hour-long re-enactment was aired on BBC Channel 4 in October of 2002. It depicted the confrontation between the pickets and the police outside the coking plant, the lines of police confronting miners, the police charges and the advance into the heart of the village. In the mélée rocks are hurled, cars are burned, and confrontations take place in front of some 3000 local witnesses.[30]

Deller's work is perhaps the most well-known re-enactment project and has been the object of some dismissive criticism. The proponent of dialogical aesthetics, Grant Kester, implied in a critique of Claire Bishop's writings on relational aesthetics that works that have a direct impact on people's lives are more significant that Deller's agonistic effort. Bishop was not so favourable to the project as she herself wrote: "Deller's event was both politically legible and utterly pointless: It summoned the experimental potency of political demonstrations but only to expose a wrong seventeen years too late."[31] In an online essay, Katie Kitamura argues for a more favourable view of Deller's "relational" work, seeing it as a worthy exercise in collective memory that contains in it not only the possibility of opening old wounds, but an unpredictability that offers the possibility of new outcomes. The recreation thus acts as a possible "uncontainment" of the original events.[32] Whereas historical societies emphasize the permanent closedness of the original events, Deller's collective project emphasizes the language of historicity and a loose melancholia.

What if, in contrast to Deller's project, a work emphasized the openness of outcomes by reducing the historical specificity of the work, and by substituting a cultural materialism for historicity? This is perhaps one way to think of the difference between *The Battle of Orgreave* and Dutch artist Aernout Mik's contribution to the 2007 Venice Biennial, the video installation *Training Ground*. For this work, Mik enlisted nonprofessional actors to play out the roles of contemporary "biopolice" in the process of arresting illegal immigrants. It is described by Mik as an *imaginary* rather than a symbolic training for how to deal with *sans-papiers* – a staging of the political imaginary. Emphasizing the Foucauldian idea of biopower and Agamben's writings on Homo Sacer, the cutator, Maria Hlavajova, places Mik's work in the context of a veritable civil war that she considers to be constitutive of the contemporary conditions of (bare) life in the West. Mik is somewhat less exacting.[33] "You cannot reduce art to its idea," he says.

> This work is not about immigration, it is not about fear, violence or national security, nor is it about staged fictional scenarios versus documentary footage from real situations. (...) If the work contains all these references ... it is with the intention of over-saturating it with unbearably weighty comments on how we can conceive the world.[34]

In contrast to Deller and his team, Mik did not do any research into how police are trained, nor did he provide any training for the actors. "I try to create dialectical images," he says, that "overcome the artificial division between people."[35] Actors can exchange roles and can act out the process as they imagine it – as dramatic, humourous, confusing or terrifying. There is no script for the piece, no rehearsal, and so the artificiality of the action emphasizes relations of mimicry and alterity. Each is interested in knowing how the other will act and react.

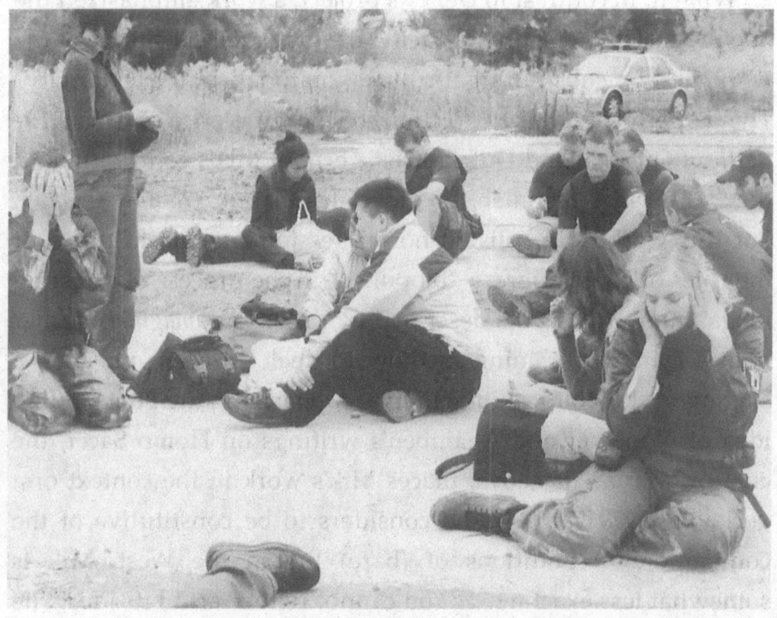

Aernout Mik, *Training Ground*, 2006. Video installation. Courtesy of World Class Boxing, Debra and Dennis Scholl Collection.

While Mik's work and notions about art have the benefit of a kind of non-deterministic openness, *Training Ground* becomes more curious and interesting than pertinent and challenging. In contrast, *The Fittest Survive* (2006), a video produced by the Austrian artist Oliver Ressler, combines both the real world gravity of a concrete social situation with the openness and non-determinacy that characterize human action and social processes. According to the statement issued by the artist, the work depicts the training services provided by a privately-owned security enterprise, a "civilian training program" for people preparing to do business in Iraq and similar crisis regions. The video follows participants while on a five-day "Surviving Hostile Regions" course that simulates conflict situations. It has much of the same unscriptedness as Mik's piece, yet, as Ressler explains in an interview:

> The film flirts with the fact that the eight participants are obviously aware that the training scenarios represent simulated realities. However, they take them very seriously and try to behave as if it was reality. There are a few sections in the film that show the different scenarios the participants went through: unexpected shell bombardments, kidnapping by a paramilitary unit, a car accident and crossing a minefield. The course was structured in such a way that the participants never knew exactly what to expect in the next hour. They were just told to walk in a particular direction and to meet a person there, and then something would happen and they had to react to it. Volkmar and I did not have any more information than the participants, so the cameraman had to react very fast and spontaneously to whatever happened, staying as close as possible to the participants, which influenced the visual appearance of the film.[36]

Ressler is unambigous, however, about the work's intent: "The crisis regions' growth markets make particularly clear that the law of market economics requires hardness and ruthlessness. This warlike character of market economics transforms life into a fight in which specific individuals face ever-higher demands for better performance."[37] The dishonest discourse of democracy and human rights, he adds, legitimizes the security ideology and the recklessly unsustainable expansion of global markets.

Abstract notions like affect, mimicry and alterity, while certainly real aspects of human interaction, have no privilege as ontological categories and should instead be provided with an epistemological status that is specific to the content and context of the work. What the three projects have in common is the

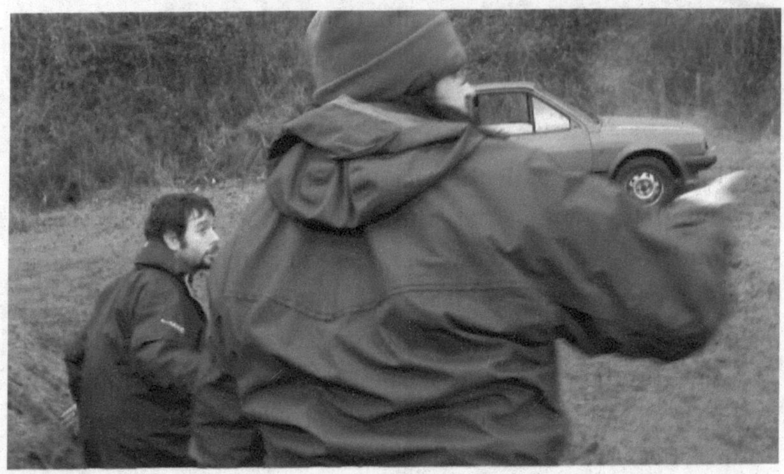

Oliver Ressler, *The Fittest Survive*, 2006. Video. Courtesy of the artist.

mixture of serious subject matter combined with the potential of fun and enjoyment. Regardless of the intentions of any of the individual works, there is always, as Theodor Adorno said of the film, a gap between intention and actual effect, especially inasmuch as the distance of autonomy is abolished. In the products of the culture industry, he argued, obscene, unofficial models of behaviour overlap with the official ones. In order to capture the consumer, the libido, "repressed by a variety of taboos," responds all the more promptly and allows the communication of whatever ideological content to pass.[38] What this means, minimally, is that affective labour or the libidinal economy, as Žižek says, "can be co-opted by different political orientations."[39] Underlying the playful or perverse role-playing that one finds in these artworks, Žižek might argue, is a fundamental prohibition: what is impossible is an actual takeover of state power in the name of revolution. Everything else is permitted. Because Black Bloc actions literally break laws, they perhaps better than most artworks allow us to consider what Žižek describes as the split law, the fact that our reality and its rules are based partly in fiction, sutured by myths and fantasies.

Consequently, what we need to assess is whether Black Bloc protesting can be effective in transforming social laws. As Adorno said about vanguard film, we should guard against taking our optimism too far. After all, the smashing of the police car on Queen Street, as everyone understood, was the perfect opportunity for everyone involved – the police who wanted to discredit the demonstrators, the onlookers hoping to catch some action, the agents provocateurs that some say had instigated the destruction, the media who were at the ready with their cameras, and even those who, after the passage of the Blocers, sat on the crushed roof of the cruiser and placed a copy of the Canadian Charter of Rights on its debris-strewn dashboard. Black Bloc actions, like the products of the culture industry, may only be promises of something they cannot deliver.

A Black Hole in Reality

As a final means of representing Black Bloc actions, and to pursue a line of questioning that addresses the relationship between anarchist culture and anarchist politics, I would like to consider the subject of culture in relation to ideology. There is no question that for many anarchists the level of ideology is distinctly that of the capitalist state. The question of ideology does not exist as a theoretical concept as such but is always already instantiated in some way in "the system." This provides anarchists with the conceit of being able to directly address what is wrong with the state of things and to always presume that their actions have immediate practical efficiency, even if they are not necessarily able to bring about the change that is desired. Instead of a theory of the logic of practice, as in the form of a critical dialectical realism, anarchists often resort to the pragmatics of common sense combined with a high-spirited moralism. Such customary sensibilities should not be dismissed, however, as we cannot do without them. They are inadequate, however, to the task of effective critique.

Marxists, in contrast, have emphasized ideology as an aspect of consciousness, as a system of ideas that creates norms of behaviour and constitutes material social processes that are later taken to be natural. The subjective aspect of ideological struggle is reflected, for instance, in Mao's view that "ideological struggle is not like other forms of struggle. The only method to be used in this struggle is that of painstaking reasoning and not crude coercion."[40] What this implies is that change can also take place at the level of cognition, or in what anarchists often rebuke as theory. It is perhaps worth remembering that after the failure of the 1848 revolutions, Marx and Engels were considered by frustrated socialists to be nothing more than counter-revolutionary and impractical literati.

On the subject of praxis, I take issue with much contemporary cultural activism that is obsessed with practice, with micro-solutions through social interaction, with every imaginable effort to replace "normal science" with the "weird," and with new models of collectivity that are deemed in every instance to be superior to work made by individual artists. I take, as a case in point, the proceedings of the roundtable conference that was published as *Critical Strategies: Perspectives on New Cultural Practices*.[41] The discussion among the participants of this conference was premised on a dissatisfaction with the state of art and activism and a sharing of ideas on how to move past what Konrad Becker referred to as bourgeois-bohemian "boutique activism." "Are we in a historical moment," asked Jim Fleming, "where art projects with social agency are really inconsequential?"[42] The fact that these questions have already been analyzed by leftists in the early twentieth century and by the sociology of culture in the postwar years does not prevent them from being posed anew in a context in which capitalist forces find new ways to manage and incite radical cultural production. Perhaps the best response to the concerns of the conference came from Critical Art Ensemble member Steve Kurtz, who made the rather commonplace assertion that the superstructural elements of society, like art, actually do matter and have a causal impact on society. Kurtz argued that in a globally developed technosphere culture becomes increasingly significant as a form of struggle and that this is reason enough to carry on with new projects. Most interestingly for us, he added that resistant cultural practices parallel direct action against the corporate-military state.[43] Certainly, in the world of media and communications, of semio-capitalism, the gap between culture and politics is attenuated. Although culture is in no way separable from the economy, it does, as a source of inherent social value, provide a place from which to offer alternatives to the mere objective of economic growth. Culture offers us, in Alain Badiou's phraseology, the possibility of living in a world in which there is concern not only for the quality of life but simply to live and to not be at the mercy of money and signs.

Wanting to live and to live better is at the core of libertarian and socialist politics. It is at the source of the expression of discontent, of actions against exploitation, of strikes, walk-outs and sit-ins. Whereas reformist unions accept endless restrictions and regulations, anarchist direct action outlines, according to Gerald Raunig, the poetry of a fictive sovereignty.[44] In Raunig's account, Black Bloc tactics are an instance of a Deleuzian swarm machine or war machine. Such a machine is opposed to structuralization and is more oriented towards non-identitarian communication, fleeing identity and state-apparatization through creative lines of flight and invention. Although it leaves unresolved the problem of a lasting revolutionary organization, he argues, the war machines seek to escape the violence of the state and the order of representation.[45] He writes:

In the appropriation of the war machine by the state apparatus, flight and invention ultimately do become war; the war machine becomes a (quasi) military apparatus. Perhaps the development of the phenomenon of the Black Bloc from Seattle 1999 to Rostock 2007 could be interpreted as this kind of process of appropriation.[46]

As Raunig is aware, the first mentions of the Black Bloc began with the mediatization and police criminalization of autonomous activists in Germany. The Bloc as such is a media construction but no less powerful because of this.

Mainstream media images can be affirmed by factions on the left, as was the case with the photographic representation of communards in the nineteenth century. According to British art historian Gen Doy, images of women and men who were active in the Paris Commune were perceived as not being in the interest of the French state. Rejecting theories of disciplinary power/knowledge, Doy argues for the idea that images embody social relations in a dialectical manner. She writes: "The consciousness of being an active subject participating in historical and social change is something that theories positing 'regimes of truth' and 'discourses' of subjectivity do little to elucidate, and much to obscure."[47] Consciousness of one's place in history and in social relations can allow people to intervene in the material conditions they live in. As material traces of the events, portrait photographs of communards were prohibited by the French state and removed from sight. Although those images were taken by photographers with commercial motives, and although they could be purchased for different reasons, communard prisoners cooperated in their manufacture in exchange for photos they could keep for themselves and interpreted them in terms of their political, social and cultural knowledge.

Doy makes the assertion that not only is structural Marxism not enough to ground images in concrete social relations, neither are the psychoanalytic theories of castration and fetishism that inform the act of looking. We could remap this onto Raunig's idea that the anarchical quality of the war machine supports capital as well as the fantasy of escape from capital. What then of psychoanalytic notions of subjectivity? If the smashed Starbucks window in some ways represents the Lacanian "name of the father," is a Black Bloc action organized around the desire for an iced cappucino its rejection?[48] Consciousness, according to psychoanalysis, is constructed out of unconscious formations and desires. Does this mean there can be no conscious resistance that is not in some way a capitulation to the laws of language-structured-like-the-unconscious? Can consciousness proceed through symbolization and the transformation of signifiers that are then put into correspondence with objective movements and necessity?[49]

According to Žižek, the subject is not only subject to external desires that are caused by various objects, signs and *things* that s/he comes into contact with, but in the shift from desire to drive, the subject also cathects desire, produces it in an intersubjective exchange. While the subject may have a goal – like smashing a window – the way that they go about doing this, their aim, is the actual purpose of the drive. Enjoyment revolves around a partial drive, that is, the social, symbolic and political process of creating actions that can enter the circuit of the subject's biological reproduction.[50] The libidinal impact of an object increases as one attempts to destroy it, as in the case of censored cultural works that gain notoriety and visibility due to their prohibition. The prohibited object thus embodies a surplus enjoyment – the Lacanian *plus de jouir*, the no-more-enjoyment that is beyond the pleasure principle and is a constituent of the reality principle.

The paradox of Black Bloc protest is its impossible relation to private property. Direct action can therefore be thought of as the impossible equivalent of exchange relations and capitalist surplus. Our deliberations in determining the effectivity of Black Bloc tactics should thus be focused on the "real of the drive" of direct action. Such actions are not premised in their immediate fulfillment but in the communication that the desire to smash capitalism can never be satisfied with such limited gestures. The desire is deeper and spreads from one symbol to another, reproducing itself towards infinity. Still, as the broken window affirms, the transgression of the symbolic Law also brings on anxiety. The only way to negotiate with this anxiety is through fantasmatic projection, which can perhaps mitigate the desire for unmediated representation. What movement activists should do is look indirectly at the smashed windows, aesthetically perhaps, with an attitude that is supported by the desire for a reality that is possible and as though the smashed window does not exist in itself but only as the materialization of capitalist distortion. Direct action, we could say, and to paraphrase Žižek once again, gives positive existence to the unreality of the world, to its incompleteness. The disproportionate irrationality of tactics and play allows for a surplus of subjective dreaming that alters the coordinates of the situation. Social democrats and news media are thus not enemies of the movement but rather only some of the mediators of the symbolic universe and the guardians of our sleep.

The Québec Maple Spring, the Red Square and After

In August of 2012 the Québec Liberal Party under Jean Charest announced a provincial election that would take place just after Labour Day and before the resumption of fall classes. The premier had presented the election as a sort of referendum in which the province was asked to vote on the student strike, which at its peak had mobilized nearly 300,000 students and which since the passing of the unconstitutional anti-strike and anti-demonstration 'Law 78' had brought into the struggle broad swathes of civil society. Student groups insisted that even if Charest lost the election, the struggle for a social strike and for free university access would continue. As it turns out the Liberals lost to the Parti Québécois, whose leader Pauline Marois announced on September 7 that she would abolish the special law and would put off tuition fee hikes for at least two years – time enough to review the matter at a future summit on postsecondary education.[1] Beginning in the month of March, students had held mass demonstrations on the 22nd of each month. Among many other forms of direct action, they also held nightly marches that began at 8:00 pm at Place Émilie-Gamelin and continued late into the evening. After the passing of the special law, the nightly marches intensified, leading to the 8:00 pm cazarolas that saw neighbours and neighbourhoods coming out to raise the stakes of the strike. On September 22nd, however, at the first major march planned for after the election, the turnout was minimal. After less than one hour, Montreal city police dispersed the few thousand people assembled. The social strike, it would seem, was only a shadow of the more tangible struggle for affordable tuition fees. While now is the time to draw some immediate lessons, it is possible to also look to past lessons as we think ahead and also as we quite rightfully celebrate a real victory.

Writing in the late 1960s and early 70s, the Italian poet, theorist and filmmaker Pier Paolo Pasolini warned the students of the New Left that their – our – insistent indignation was, in the context of a "homologizing" consumer culture, not a form of engagement, but a means to live with a clear conscience. Its features, he thought, were best expressed by the civil rights and student resistance movements that had developed in the United States. Its "negative characteristic," he argued, was its lack of class consciousness.[2] In the country of democratic radicalism, vindication of the exploited needed the mediation of idealism; it filled the vacuum of communism with moralism rather than realism, with spiritualism rather than revolt. Yet, for all that, the "anti-community" of Students for a Democratic Society and of the Student Nonviolent Coordinating Committee reminded Pasolini of the wartime Resistance movement.

Today, as the crises of capitalism are once again generating indignation, the amorphous forms of a faceless global biopower continue to blur the distinctions between the intelligentsia, the technocratic class, the ruling class and the working majority.[3] The symptom of such "democratic materialism," as Alain Badiou refers to it, is not only democracy, but more pragmatically, *empowerment*.[4] The radical struggle against neoliberal capitalism today no longer calls for class conscious political organization, but for forms of empowerment that are often not a threat to the productive goals of global capitalism. In his interpretation of Badiou, Bruno Bosteels writes:

Politics as a procedure of truth, however, cannot be reduced to the typically youthful protest against the eternally oppressive and corrupt nature of the state apparatus. (...) A militant subject emerges only when the particular terms of the various memberships that define society are put down and abolished in favor of a generic concept of truth as universally the same for all. Politics, in other words, has nothing to do with respect for difference or for the other, not even the absolute other, and everything to do with equality and sameness. (...) By traversing and deposing the different representations of identity with which the excess of state power maintains itself in its very errancy, a political procedure gradually begins to revolve around the notion of a generic set, that is, a set without determining attributes or qualities.[5]

A democratic empowerment is certainly the vision that one draws from the July manifesto of the CLASSE (*La Coalition large de l'Association pour une solidarité syndicale étudiante*), the student coalition that along with the FECQ (*Fédération étudiante collégiale du Québec*) and FEUQ (*Fédération étudiante universitaire du Québec*) spearheaded the *printemps érable*, the québécois version of the popular demonstrations, assemblies and occupations that have given expression to recent leftist struggles, from the revolutions of the Arab Spring, to the Greek and Spanish encampments, to the Wisconsin uprising and the Occupy movements that first erupted in New York City.[6] To refer to only this one tract by what is considered to be the most radical of the student groups is perhaps not at all representative of a situation that brings together anarchists, social democrats, left liberals, socialists and communists alike. A more pragmatic description of "associated institutions," and certainly one that would come closer to the CLASSE's general "social movements" outlook, could corre-spond instead to David Harvey's list of non-governmental organizations, anarchist and autonomous grassroots organiza-tions, traditional left political parties and unions, social movements guided by the pragmatic need to resist displacement and dispossession, and lastly, minority and identitarian movements. He considers communist anyone who understands and struggles against the destructive tendencies of capitalism.[7]

Given all of this one wonders why it is that the students have chosen the red square as their symbol. Having first emerged as a symbol of Québec student politics in 2005 (previously associated with struggles against poverty within the Québec National Assembly), the red square could be compared to the cardboard signs of Occupy Wall Street, promissory notes that Gregory Sholette has described as "an obligation to a future reader from a place already dislocated in time."[8] However, if the cardboard signs, the wired downtown encampments and the general assemblies somehow seem novel, the symbolism of the red square makes it such that it is we today who are this "future reader" whose obligation, it seems to me, refers to a distinctly communist trajectory. The red square and the manifesto: are these dehistoricized postmodern signs, avatars of a collective amnesia, or something more like the objects of a Situationist *détournement*, richer in constructive possibilities than presumed by the myth of progress? If the latter is closer to the truth, this usage of the red square nevertheless considers the Situationist moment as one that is to be repeated, since, in no way is it possible to confirm that today's revolutionaries have effectively condemned "all the ado of the lecture halls and classrooms as mere *noise*, verbal pollution."[9]

Amidst all of this academic noise is certainly the belief that we have not finished with postmodernism and its hasty obituary on the end of ideological meta-narratives. The denial that postmodernism has been eclipsed by neoliberal globalization affects both the realms of culture and politics. If it makes little sense for us today to ponder the forms of culture that correspond to globalization, it would make equally little sense for us to be overly concerned with the forms of culture that are specific to anti-capitalist protest movements. The point, as the saying goes, is to change the world. When one talks about the disappearance of art's reified status in terms of bourgeois autonomy, however, about the sublation of art and life, one usually thinks of the Russian avant-gardes. In particular, one thinks of Kazimir

Malevich's *Black Square* of 1913, hung like an icon in his *Last Futurist Exhibition* and defined by him as the "zero of form," a transitional image whose shift from white ground to black figure represented the passage from the individual bourgeois self to that of a new collectivity. When Malevich was invited by Chagall to the Art Institute in Vitebsk, his lessons in Suprematist radical abstraction were quickly adopted by a group of communist artists who assembled under the name of UNOVIS. The leader of the group, El Lissitzky, adopted Malevich's use of geometric shapes and incorporated these into his designs for posters, books, buildings and exhibitions. Unlike Malevich, Lissitzky's "Prouns" were shapes that led from 2D to 3D, with multiple perspectives and shifting axes. The Proun work by Lissitzky that most dramatically incorporates the red square is his 1920-21 *New Man*, a graphic design for a remake of the Futurist play *Victory Over the Sun*. The ideal of UNOVIS was to organize and collectivize work, rather than embellish art. While working as a cultural ambassador to the Republic of Weimar, Lissitzky made use of the new printing techniques of a Hanover firm. The colour palette for his *New Man* was red and black, the same colours that are emblazoned in his well-known pieces *Beat the Whites with the Red Wedge* (1919) and *Monument to Rosa Luxemburg* (1919-21).

El Lissitzky's work lent symbolic support to the communist "reds" during a protracted civil war against the monarchists, conservatives, liberals and socialists alike. This association of communism with violence is prevalent today as one of the most heightened ideological features of liberal political blackmail. As Bosteels recently put it, "from all sides we are bombarded with calls to live up to our duty to remember the past disasters of humanity, lest history repeat itself." More often than not, he adds, "this inflation of memory comes at the cost of postponing a genuinely critical history of ourselves from the point of view of the present."[10] Consider as an example of such a postponement Grant Kester's essays on the similarities between vanguard intellectuals and avant-garde artists.[11] In both cases, Kester argues, the radical seeks to reveal "the 'true' nature of domination" through *its* "exemplary consciousness." It does this, he says, by exaggerating the suffering of the working class or multitude and provoking the repressive apparatus of the bourgeois state. The ensuing conflict and further suffering of the working class is justified, he says, by the utopian belief that this will lead to "total emancipation." The upshot for Kester, who writes this in relation to contemporary collaborative art practices, is that the vanguard conforms to a "dyadic structure" in which it is supposed to bring unenlightened viewers (both the bourgeois and the working class) to a higher level of consciousness. Notwithstanding the fact that Kester considers class to be a matter of identity, an understanding that dismisses Marx's theory of contradiction, does his description not perfectly describe the situation that has erupted in relation to the student strike? Did the mass demonstrations, the nightly demonstrations, the bridge obstructions, metro smoke bomb scares, the office raids and broken bank windows not lead to the imposition of the draconian Law 78? Did the Québec Liberal Party not repeatedly denounce the student movement, and was the students' chosen symbol, the red square, not associated with "violence and intimidation."[12] The fact that Kester proposes no radical solutions to the effects of capitalism should give us some pause as to the political consequences of the fear that is evoked by the repressive power of the state.[13] Today's radicalism has indeed been conditioned by a hegemonic shift of power. If, as Pasolini asserts, the working class once knew itself to be different from and opposed to the bourgeois class, today's leftists know themselves as mostly different from communists – which is to suggest that to a great extent they do not know themselves.

Bosteels tells us that in today's context in which everything is fodder for historicization and in which capitalist ideology emphasizes difference, multiplicity and perpetual change, we should refuse to mourn communism. Communism remains untimely, he says, dialectically historical and nonhistorical. Bosteels' idea of the actuality of communism fits nicely with Slavoj Žižek's four reasons to preserve the idea of communism: because this tradition remains the tradition of authentic popular struggles for emancipation; because today's problems are problems of the commons; because other terms, like democracy, socialism and justice are easily appropriated by the right; and lastly, because we are approaching dangerous times in which we may have to do things on a mass scale, perhaps even violent things, while avoiding both principled opportunism and the totalitarian temptation.[14] The red square, unlike the cardboard signs, has so far had the advantage of being associated with the power of organized structures. Here is a social form that is not about empowerment based on identity, but based on universal, emancipatory organization. Against the abstract background of debt and the threat of crippling fines for those who dared to pursue the strike, the red square has not only had a symbolic but an iconic value, one that promised and will continue to promise a revolutionary transformation of society.

Globalization and the Politics of Culture:
An Interview with Imre Szeman

What is the role of culture in an era of globalization? This is one of the questions that animates the work of Imre Szeman, founder of the Canadian Association of Cultural Studies and Canada Research Chair in Cultural Studies at the University of Alberta. Szeman's thinking combines a strong appreciation of the critical potential of cultural studies work with an understanding of the importance of Marxist theory, especially at this critical moment in human history. With the end of national culture as a framework for progress in the arts, culture becomes increasingly tied to the new master narrative, he says, of the traumas of globalization. As culture's agenda is increasingly set by the operations of global capital, it becomes imperative, he argues, to create an imaginative vocabulary that can challenge biocapitalism's fantasy of endless accumulation. While globalization democratizes the imagination, creating new identities and new public spheres, for Szeman, it simultaneously shifts our focus away from culture – the predominant aesthetic and representational condition of postmodernism – towards macro-political issues. In this context, he says, class struggle reasserts itself, political economy returns with a vengeance, and even the immanent aesthetic of workerist theory seems to pale in comparison with the transcendent mediation of radical contestation.

Whereas the theorists of empire, Michael Hardt and Antonio Negri, argue that desire must become practical, that joyful communitarianism must of necessity replace the "fanatical ethical purity" of revolutionary theory, Szeman emphasizes the fact that this immediacy of desire is largely a result of biopolitical cultural production, which, while it causes a mutation of capitalism, is nevertheless fueled by older, basic processes of resource extraction and the industrial exploitation of wage labour. If globalization implies that culture's relative autonomy is unsustainable, Szeman proposes that we should fight to win spaces of autonomy, that revolution holds more promise for us than the evolutionary anti-art of exodus. Against the fetishization of theoretical novelty, Szeman therefore suggests that the imaginative resources of cultural resistance are readily at hand and all it takes for us to imagine an after to globalization is the return to a strategic realism that is willing to confront the limitations and arbitrariness of neoliberal economics.

After a lecture he gave in Montreal in March 2011, I asked Szeman for an interview, the outcome of which produced more questions and more topics than we could reasonably manage in one text. Over several months we corresponded by email and he kindly endeavoured to provide responses to a few questions.

Marc James Léger: In your essay "Imagining the Future: Globalization, Postmodernism and Criticism," you argue that the idea of the artist as a vanguard is definitely over and that this is a good thing.[1] Art and politics proceed today with uncertainty, you say. I was particularly interested in this essay with the simple way that you contrast postmodernism with globalization. Globalization is less about aesthetics and cultural representation and has more to do with an agenda set for culture by global capital. Could you tell us how it is that you came up with this solution to post-postmodernism? Also, could you say more about this predominance of capitalist globalization and how you might respond to a thinker like Nicolas Bourriaud who is eager to understand the mode of aesthetics that corresponds to this new era.[2] I wonder if you think there is any space for an avant-garde articulation of culture in this context.

Imre Szeman: The relationship between art and politics is indeed uncertain – or so it seems to me. The gestures of many of those art works (and artists) explicitly committed to political engagement and change are towards little more than simply difference from the present rather than some (aesthetically or politically) well-articulated interrogation of system and structure. In art as in other areas of our social life, we exist at a moment in which political ideas adequate to the present are in short supply. Despite all manner of social inequality and political obscenities done in the name of democracy, a broad swathe of the planet's population has come to accept that the primary function of the state is to run itself out of business. After 2008, neoliberalism exists less as ideology than as habit – an increasingly common ready-to-hand vocabulary of quotidian complaint about public waste that supposedly can only be cured by private pragmatism, whatever the consequences to public life. The inadequacies of the state as a result of the reduction of its services only confirms the veracity of this social narrative – a closed spiral of cause and effect that has proven to be enormously difficult to challenge or unsettle.

I don't need to rehearse the now long and persistent attacks that have been carried out on the idea or ideal of the avant garde that lent to the practice of art a revolutionary potential. The collapse of the autonomy of art as a result of the expansion of mass culture – a process described authoritatively by Peter Bürger – is viewed by some critics as cause for alarm and by others as no big deal.[3] The alarm? Only through its relative autonomy from capitalism could art offer a challenge to it. However, this very possibility tended to occlude the fact that its autonomy left it always already separate from the quotidian in a manner that meant it could not truly intervene in capitalist culture. There is still another response to this configuration of the power of art, which is to view the original formulae by which art is assigned its potentially powerful autonomy as something like a category mistake, which is why its eclipse is seen as no big deal. This is certainly true of the work of Pierre Bourdieu, for whom aesthetic judgement acts as a euphemism that underwrites and enables social distinctions, and little more.[4] It is true, too, of Jacques Rancière's intervention into the relationship between aesthetics and politics, which reconfigures it in yet another way: art as a specific form of work on the "distribution of the sensible," a field in which politics proper acts as well. The rupture or break once associated with vanguardist imaginings of the aesthetic are in this schema muted, to say the least. In *The Politics of Aesthetics*, for instance, Rancière writes,

> the arts only ever lend to projects of domination or emancipation what they are able to lend them, that is to say, quite simply, what they have in common with them: bodily positions and movements, functions of speech, parceling out of the visible and the invisible. Furthermore, the autonomy they can enjoy or the subversion they can claim credit for rest on the same foundation.[5]

To me this view is not so far removed from the "relational aesthetics" championed by Nicolas Bourriaud, though he lacks anything like the politico-aesthetic structure Rancière has elaborated around visibility/sensibility and equality.[6] I'm inclined to agree with Hal Foster's critique that Bourriaud's aesthetics amounts to little more than a "shaky analogy between an open work and an inclusive society, as if a desultory form might evoke a democratic community, or a non-hierarchical installation predict an egalitarian world."[7]

I have a slightly different take on the eclipse of artist as a vanguard. If Bourdieu sees the politics hitherto associated with the aesthetic as bad sociology and Rancière views it as something akin to sloppy political philosophy, what strikes me with especial force are the impacts of historical shifts in dominant discourses on the social significance of art and aesthetics. In "Imagining the Future," several things emerge from a comparison of postmodernism and globalization as dominant narratives. The postmodern was an aesthetic category before it became a larger descriptor of an epistemic or ontological condition. Globalization, on the other hand, seems to have little to do with culture or aesthetics *per se*. When one says 'global culture' it is to affirm the realities that postmodernism only hinted at rather than to name a specific artistic or architectural mode or style. With globalization, the emphasis is directly on the restructuring of relations of politics and power, on the rescaling of economic production from the national to the transnational, on the light speed operations of finance capital, and on the societal impacts of the explosive spread of information technologies – no need for any complex symptomatology! Finally, globalization is a dominant discourse with a much stronger public presence than postmodernism. Social and political struggles occur over the ideologies and imperatives of globalization in a way that they never did in postmodernism – more is at stake, and more directly so. One of things that I argue for in "Imagining the Future" and elsewhere is that this shift in dominant social narratives away from culture to a blunter, cruder argument about the nature of power is a sign of an evacuation of the power of art and culture. Dominance once required an investment in the practices and discourses of art and culture, including the humanities in universities; now power seems less anxious about having a purchase on this terrain – it's no longer where power is lived and consolidated. This has to do, of course, with social and technological developments that have led to a commodification of images, which is, in the words of Fredric Jameson, "why it is vain to expect a negation of the logic of the commodity production from it," as well as the different relationship to culture generated by mass culture – a development narrated by many thinkers, from Guy Debord to Jameson himself.[8]

Does this mean that art and cultural production once had a power that has completely evaporated in the context of globalization? This is how many critics seem to read the situation. But isn't this to fix art at a specific moment in time – an avant-garde moment whose politics are already in question in any case?

Doesn't art, too, change in conjunction with broader social developments? Mikkel Bolt Rasmussen has recently suggested that while much art practice remains complicit with established powers, "at the same time it is important to point out that the space of art is still characterized by the presence of various representations of the political and attempts to use the field of art as a starting point for the visualization of conflicts that have been marginalized in the broader mainstream public sphere."[9] It's a mistake to write off the political possibilities of art; it's a mistake, too, to imagine it to be more than a sideshow in the ebb and flow of global capital – that is, as a site at which one might expect wholesale political change. It might seem a banal point, but it has to be made: it's 2011, not 1911.

MJL: Indeed, it's not 1911 and by all accounts we're in a world of biopolitical governance. However, I completely agree with Alain Badiou when he argues that certain sequences and events cannot be limited to specific dates – for example, the idea of that communism died a very certain death in 1989.[10] A specific sequence has come to a close but this does not condemn us to a post-traumatic complicity either. We can have anxieties about affirmative culture or about recuperation but that's not all there is. One can look at this in very pragmatic terms to say that socialism is not something that exists only in China and Cuba, but that many social programs, environmental and labour regulations that we benefit from here in Canada are the products of socialist ideas and endeavours. By the same token, if autonomous art has been falsely sublated into culture industry, as Bürger says, we can nevertheless find avant-garde forms of resistance to capitalist domination that are not on the same order as the postmodern politics of representation. I wouldn't say "good riddance" to the idea of the avant-garde anymore than I would say it to the idea of communism. And if there is to be an after to capitalist globalization, I can't personally imagine how Marx wouldn't have something to do with getting there.

In terms of what I wanted to bring up with regard to Bourriaud's idea of the "altermodern," what I meant to ask you about is the eagerness with which cultural theorists may want to wish away the problems associated with economic globalization, least of all its implications for neoliberal policy, and bring the focus back to culture. The particular form that this takes today is that of variations on the idea of pluralism: difference, hybridity, transnationalism, multiculturalism, diaspora, cosmopolitanism. In the same essay, "Imagining the Future," you argue that the agenda that is set for culture is informed by the operations of global capital and that this has become a new master narrative. Is the culturalization of politics that one finds in postmodern discourse in any way challenged by the return to political economy and class analysis? By the way, I don't think that Bourdieu thought that politics associated with aesthetic ideology was bad sociology, but rather the outcome of a particular class habitus, which had to do with his appreciation of the concept of totality. As I see things what we have today is an ascendance of petty bourgeois allodoxia in which the lifestyle concerns of an international class refuses all determinations in matters of identity and so we have a clear shift from national culture to global petty bourgeois culture.

IS: I don't think that anything I suggested above means "good riddance"! Questioning the specific politico-aesthetic configuration associated with the historical avant garde is intended to get us past a (still, it must be said) widely held feeling that the connection between art and politics is over and done with – over and done with because it is thought to be able to operate in a certain way (now gone) and no other. I agree: this doesn't mean we have to wallow in the certitudes of affirmative culture. It does mean, however, that we have to address new circumstances head on.

With respect to the focus on culture in contemporary thought, there are two related but importantly different claims being made here. The first has to do with a focus on culture as opposed to analyses of political economy or class; the second asks a question about the nature of that focus – what you here describe correctly as variations on ideas about the importance of pluralism. I don't think one can avoid assessments and analyses of everything that constitutes 'culture.' The social world is legible only through the discourses and narratives that constitute it. Capitalism is one of these, as is, say, the varied discourses of governmentality that comprise the 'rational' and efficient organization of populations at the present time. This is not to say that all cultural or social discourses operate with equal force or importance, or that some cluster of them shouldn't be taken as a politico-social axiomatic that offers a key to what is happening to us now. But nor is it to say that those elements determined to be axiomatic are plainly and clearly the dominant site of power 'in the last instance' – the kind of idea that legitimates reductive or vulgar analyses of all kinds. We sometimes forget why there was a cultural turn in the first place, which has to do with the reshaping of everyday life in the context of mass culture and new technologies of communication and information, and the consequent impact of this turn on epistemologies and ontologies of the social and political. *Nothing* social or political is given immediately to sensation; we have to comprehend it through the web of desires, beliefs, information and affect that constitutes 'culture' today. If this is the case, we can't possibly avoid thinking about culture.

My objection is that as important as culture is, there is also a tendency of cultural theorists to overvalue it – to not even be tempted to vulgarly assert the significance of economics or political structure, since they don't recognize the importance of these factors for culture to begin with, and because their concern begins and starts with cultural objects whose significance for analyses is framed not by a problem to be solved, but by traditions of analysis within institutions of higher education. The pressures and politics of the latter also tend to generate analyses that have to place novelty or innovation at the heart of critical writing – the discernment in this or that piece of fiction or work of art of, for instance, the secret to the entire system of capitalism, or just as frequently, of a model of political engagement one doesn't find in the world at large. The impact of culture on social epistemologies doesn't mean that one should wallow in culture, or that knowledge as such is now impossible (as one variant of postmodernism suggests), but that our sense of the world and its operations have of necessity to be complex and multi-layered.

As to the second point: insofar as hybridity, transnationalism, multiculturalism, diaspora, etc., draw attention to the operations of power vis-à-vis the management of difference, the shaping of populations through movement in space (or the prevention of such movement), impediments to social possibility and mobility due to cultural, social and racial differences, etc., these are valuable concepts with which to understand globalization. My anxiety is that often enough such concepts are deployed in the absence of an analysis of the operations of identity and difference *within* capitalism; such a politics as does exist is often unreflexively liberal, connected mainly to the dynamics of political and social tolerance and the extension of rights but without a larger consideration of the imperatives of global capital. As long as it can extract surplus, difference isn't a problem for capital (though it obviously is for the older formations of nation and nationalism). Indeed, as many critics have pointed out, pluralism and difference are today powerful ideas guiding and organizing the practices of consumption and consumerism.

I wouldn't bundle 'cosmopolitanism' into these pluralistic terms. The criticisms of cosmopolitanism tend to be that it *isn't* particularistic or pluralistic, but that in its presumed universalism it is far too limiting a concept. There are liberal cosmopolitanisms (such as Daniele Archibugi's) that see the concept as little more than the name for international political schemes that would address problems that are global rather than national in scale.[11] Tim Brennan's suggestion that we can already take "contemporary neoliberal orthodoxy as a form of unofficial party organization across national frontiers" is pretty much all one has to say in response to Archibugi's "cosmopolitical democracy project."[12]

But it is possible to use cosmopolitanism as a powerful regulative and political ideal – as something akin to how equality works in Rancière's thought. This is, it seems to me, how it first appears in Immanuel Kant's "Perpetual Peace." The first two of the three definitive articles of perpetual peace echo Archibugi's aims by laying the groundwork for a formally instituted international body that would be the managing political organ of a federation of independent nation states, each established on the basis of a republican constitution (think today of the UN or IMF). The third and final definitive article ("Cosmopolitan Right Shall Be Limited to Conditions of Universal Hospitality") attempts to identify a right that all people should have everywhere – a *universal* right. Universal hospitality means that a stranger who arrives on someone else's territory must be treated peaceably if they themselves are not hostile. The reason for this? Kant writes:

All men are entitled to present themselves in the society of others by virtue of their right to communal possession of the earth's surface. Since the earth is a globe, they cannot disperse over an infinite area, but must necessarily tolerate one another's company. And no one originally has any greater right than anyone else to occupy any particular portion of the earth. The community of man is divided by uninhabitable parts of the earth's surface such as oceans and deserts, but even then, the *ship* or the *camel* (the ship of the desert) make it possible for them to approach their fellows over these ownerless tracts, and to utilize as a means of social intercourse that *right to the earth's surface* which the human race shares in common.[13]

This strikes me as an important and radical claim, and it is one that seems to go against almost everything else that Kant writes in "Perpetual Peace." The right to the earth's surface – a right that necessitates universal hospitality for those crossing borders – does not supersede the fact that claims *have been* made to this or that patch of the earth, and that hospitality has to be *granted* by owner to visitor, by citizen to foreigner. However much in Kant's view nations might in the future be held together in an increasingly powerful international federation, underwritten by increasingly universal laws that apply to everyone, the borders between nation states appear to remain fixed. At times, Kant simply presumes the inevitable existence of nations; at other times, he argues for their necessity: nations can't or shouldn't intermingle due to linguistic and religious differences produced by nature (through a kind of geographic determinism); or nations shouldn't be brought under a single power, because "laws progressively lose their impact as government increases its range."[14] Nature separates humanity into nations, and does so, according to Kant, "wisely" because the leader of a single earthly nation could only ever be a despot. As a root universal principle, all of humanity can claim the right to all of the globe; the reality of the situation – which is seen by Kant less as something unfortunate than as a productive and valuable state of affairs – is that borders create strangers, and to strangers we owe little more than hospitality. If we take cosmopolitanism to be the right to universal access, however, it places a demand that a justification be made in every situation where such access doesn't exist, a demand we can turn on Kant himself. The articulation of a right to the earth's surface in the same passage in which the universality of this right is undercut by the assertion of a need to tolerate visitors goes to the heart of the problems and limits of the liberal rights regimes that manage our legal and political affairs today.

Can we not say that political art makes a similar demand, engaging in a conceptual and political game that asks why *this* and not *that*? It might not be a demand that is answered by society at large; it is important, however, that such demands which pierce to the heart of the organization of power are made, and, to bring it back around to where your question started, this of necessity goes beyond the limits that still adhere to how we tend to understand 'culture.'

MJL: The problem with affirmative culture is not that one might wallow in it, it's rather, as I understand Adorno and Marcuse, that it allows us to forget suffering and at the same time it might also, as is evident in some forms of progressive culture, seek to satiate audiences with moral indignity and sentimentality without imparting any useful sense of how a situation could be subjectivized. In other words, the criticism of affirmative culture is not what it allows in terms of pleasure, it's what it doesn't allow in terms of equality, truth, justice. I tend to agree with your description of cosmopolitanism, though I am concerned to distinguish class politics from cosmopolitics, which promotes legal notions of human rights that act in tandem with the developmentalist aspects of economic globalization and military incursion. I think that it could be useful to propose a triangulation of culture, politics and economy, and avoid what anarchist thought and media studies often do, which is, when speaking about culture and politics, to collapse social relations with means of production, or to assume that culture, even social practice, is directly political. This is to say that we should allow culture a certain measure of effectivity and even of autonomy with regard to both politics and economics.

What you say about hospitality relates in some ways to what I alluded to in terms of petty bourgeois allodoxia and biocapitalism. Progressives are enthralled at the moment with models of culture that propose various ways that social subjects should change their structures of feeling through affective bonding, stranger intimacy, tolerance towards the other and towards the stranger within ourselves, etc., with variations on ideas borrowed from Bergsonian models of creative evolution or Levinasian ethics which are then linked to various political agendas. Most often these anti-revolutionary reformist models make use of very naive or idealist notions of social engineering that are not unlike counter-cultural models from past decades and which typically exclude class analysis. This to me is an indication of the ascendance of petty bourgeois culture, as it's understood for example by Giorgio Agamben in his book *The Coming Community*.[15] The problem here is that in this cultural context left militancy is made to stand in for everything that is universalizing, masculinist, totalizing, and so on. This attitude tends to avoid complex uses of the notions of totality, rationality, subjectivity, and universality that are in fact necessary if we are to pursue a politics of universal emancipation.

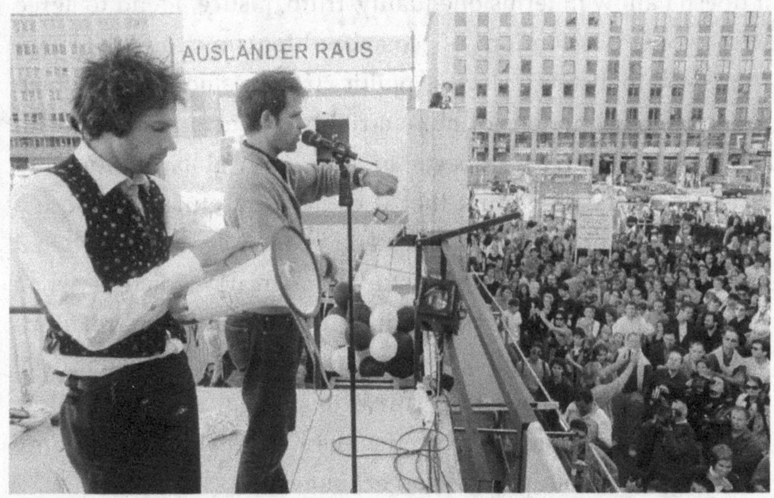

Christoph Schlingensief, *Bitte liebt Österreich! (Please Love Austria)*, 2000. Performance event. Photo © David Baltzer/bildbuehne.de.

With reference to what you discussed, an interesting example of critical public art is that of Christoph Schlingensief's *Bitte liebt*

Österreich! (Please Love Austria!) of 2000. The artist organized an outdoor "Big Brother" type reality show in which the Austrian public was asked to vote for which asylum seeker should be allowed to stay in the country and which should be deported. The participants were kept in a container camp that was marked *Ausländer Raus* (foreigners out!), which was meant to stage the popularity of extreme right-wing ideas in Austria and the state's recognition of the right populist FPÖ party of Jörg Haider. In many ways Schlingensief's work anticipated the violent acts of Anders Behring Breivik in Norway and the communication of sympathy for his ideas on behalf of neo-fascist groups in France and Italy, not to mention the exploitation by the mainstream media of anti-Muslim rhetoric. In less drastic terms, this also reflects immigration policies in Canada and the U.S. that are meant to detract from scrutiny of labour policy, industrial relations, and the like.

My next question then relates specifically to your essay "Marxist Literary Criticism, Then and Now," which was published in the journal *Mediations* in 2009.[16] In this piece you state that there are three basic modes of Marxist art criticism: (1) reminders to historicize and to focus on class and political economy, (2) critiques of the institutions of cultural production and analysis, and (3) anxieties about affirmative culture and critique of the cultural studies tendency to find moments of resistance in almost anything. I'm wondering, with reference to your recent collaboration with Eric Cadzyn, *After Globalization*, if there is still some room within critical theory for the analysis of the transition to communism and also if there is anything left of the Marxist-Leninist-Maoist experiment with political organization.[17] In other words, it seems to me that if class struggle is to reassert itself and if "political economy is back in style," which indeed it is, art criticism should have something to say about political organization. I ask this question knowing very well that in the contemporary visual arts at least there is enormous energy

being dedicated to organization in relation to new class compositions. Most of this, however, tends to be devised in terms of
utopian and small-scale anarchist models, which the international class of capitalists, the state bureaucracies and their
military-police apparatuses are hardly worried about. How then
can (2) spend less time worrying about (3) and do more to be
useful to (1) and what do you think the role of cultural studies is
in this age of post-politics, austerity capitalism and the corporatization of the university?

IS: These are good points to make. Certain concepts come
loaded with meanings that, as a result of their histories, cannot be
easily shaken off. And so cosmopolitanism does speak to human
rights regimes and developmental schema, even if at its core it
names a possibility of affiliations and connections that go beyond
national sentiment or the prohibitions of a lifeworld organized
around property. As those theorists who draw attention to
negative cosmopolitanisms make clear, all too often discourses of
cosmopolitanism legitimate imperialistic and hegemonic intru-
sions by the powerful into spaces they want to manage and
control. Narratives of human rights, of economic and social
development, and (more lately) of globalization appeal to univer-
salistic measures of the human *as such*, against which the state of
this or that part of the world can be assessed. Given the imperatives and desires of the forces that are creating and promoting
these measures, it comes as little surprise that the universalism
they promote is suspect.

As for the effectivity and autonomy of culture: this, too, is a
good point to make. If I tend to err in the other direction it is
because culture is more often than not viewed as fully
autonomous (in both critical thought and in society at large), and
so reminders of limits, blocks and conditions of possibility can't
help but introduce important considerations into the discussions
of the 'what' and 'why' of culture. And I take your point about the
fear of notions such as totality and universality. As I said above,

there's no question that appeals to universality made by some thinkers (for example, liberals such as Kwame Anthony Appiah or Martha Nussbaum) have to be read with a critical eye. At the same time, a complete rejection of universality – as something akin to a category mistake when it comes to the rich diversity of human Being – is in fact a perverse affirmation of that universality which already exists: the universality of capitalist subjectivity. In an era that has been described as one in which the hitherto formal subsumption of labour under capital has become real, we already have a universal subject – an exploited subject, lacking in rights, who endures, as David Harvey puts it, "the meaningless and alienating qualities of so many jobs and so much of daily life in the midst of immense but unevenly distributed potentiality for human flourishing."[18]

Is there room for an analysis of a transition to communism? One hopes so. Is there anything left of experiments with political organization? There are. I think immediately of Erik Olin Wright's *Envisioning Real Utopias* (2010) as an example of a recent book that unapologetically devotes itself to framing emancipatory social possibilities, or of the 2006 documentary *The Power of Community: How Cuba Survived Peak Oil*, which examines the country's imaginative, collective response to the loss of more than half of its oil imports.[19] Though it is perhaps too easy to be cynical about the significance of contemporary visual arts in its explorations of political organization, I agree with you that the visual arts *are* a site in which this issue of organizational possibility is being posed and examined. However the arts might be greeted by the capitalist class, however they might be contained and consigned to spaces of relative predictability, the conceptual experimentations of the visual arts remain a genuine resource – *especially* as so many artists and art collectives move beyond lingering modernist interrogations of the nature and subject of art, and simply enact scenarios and carry out social investigations to see what these might reveal or produce. I like Hal

Foster's recent reading of the work of Thomas Hirschhorn, for instance. Foster sees Hirschhorn's work as consisting of explorations of precarity, expenditure, and of the conceptual difficulty of reading the present (the mode of the *bête* in Hirschhorn's work, who operates within the social circumstances of emergency); the resources Hirschhorn draws upon in doing so are those "that lie dormant in the 'general intellect' of the multitude, a multitude that, to different degrees, faces a state of emergency today."[20] Here we have an artist engaged in an exploration of the fundamental problems of organization today: a socioeconomic system governed by fear and insecurity, as well as a helplessness in the face of everything from the scale of existing infrastructure (from the military-security apparatus to our sheer dependence on technology) to looming ecological crises; a world premised on narratives and fantasies of growth that will have to re-build itself around perpetual lack; and finally, a historical moment of confused epistemologies which are hurt rather than helped by the enormous amounts of data we are so adept at generating. Foster describes Hirschhorn's use of everyday materials and techniques as the "search for a nonexclusive public, a public after the apparent dissolution of the public sphere."[21] That seems to be a good description of where many of us find ourselves at the moment when it comes to confronting the problem of political organization.

The question you end with about cultural studies is a big one. I refuse to write off the university, despite its many problems and limits. It remains a central site of knowledge production and legitimation; it is a space in which a large part of the population in Western countries (and an increasingly large part in the rest of the world: non-Western students now make up more than half of the globe's university population) spends a key point in their lives, a place in which the passage to (an imagined) full citizenship takes place alongside an immersion in social and political codes and beliefs. There are numerous other sites at which such social pedagogy takes place – everywhere from the communications media to spaces of religion. Still, the university matters, even if different parts of it might matter to different degrees, and even if it is not the sole political-social-cultural arbiter.

And so, in this context, is it not important to have an approach to culture that is (ideally) self-reflective about its practice as a mode of knowledge production (and indeed, clear about the need to consider the status and function of an institution such as the university within this practice), that looks at the full range of sites and spaces in which meaning is communicated (and the subject and social are produced), that explores with students the kinds of questions we've been raising in our own discussion, and finally, that might take as its subject post-politics, austerity capitalism and the corporatization of the university (and so what it can to provide students with the concepts to understand these developments)?

On the other hand I can't help but worry that the embrace of cultural studies within universities – to the limited degree that this has happened – is evidence of some of the pressures faced by the contemporary university. Raymond Williams famously identified three elements of culture: dominant, residual and emergent.[22] The arts and humanities within universities reflect the dominant values of society, though they are also importantly residual insofar as their configuration represents a different social formation than that of the present. Within the relative autonomy that exists for many of those operating within universities, should we not instead try to occupy the position of the emergent? At their very best, cultural studies are driven by the imperative to do just this.

MJL: I agree with you about the need to affirm the mediating role of institutions. Universities definitely contribute to the creation of social values and creative industry advocates typically ignore this educational contribution that the welfare state makes to the general economy. If I could ask you one last question, I would be interested in knowing what kinds of policy issues are foremost in your mind at this moment in both the national situation and in terms of globalization. With the re-election of the Harper conservatives in 2011 and the arrival of Sun News, many in the various arts sectors in Canada are expecting the state to push culture further in the direction of a commercial and free market orientation – the kind of policy offensive that we've seen recently with the memorandum put out by the Dutch State Secretary for Culture. George Yúdice makes the observation that in the context of globalization, and even if the neoliberal state maintains public funding for culture, "culture-as-resource" acts as an expedient, both in terms of economic stimulus and with regard to the management of social conflicts.[23] The exemption of culture from free trade deals like NAFTA has proven to be something of a myth, however, and this is borne out in some respects as culture wars replace notions of national culture, or dovetail with it. Yúdice argues that trade liberalization has made culture more of a protagonist than it ever was. Beyond what you've already said about cosmopolitanism and universal access, what do you think of this special place of culture in the midst global class polarization and proletarianization? Are the free traders correct? Is culture the ultimate commodity? I ask you this in part because our first meeting was in Montreal in March on the occasion of a lecture you gave at the Sauvé Scholars Foundation that was provocatively titled "Why We Don't Need Creativity."

IS: Let me talk first about why I don't think we need creativity. The 'we' is not just the left, or cultural producers, but *everyone*. And it isn't that we don't need novelty, or innovation, or change, or radical insights or interventions: it's creativity specifically that I think we don't need. I argue that creativity has become not just an empty honorific (the kind of thing that one says in praise of one's children) but also a dangerous one. It is a concept that is imagined as lying at the heart of artistic and cultural activity.

Over the course of the twentieth century, but with special force during the past two decades of globalization discourse, creativity has also come to be associated with any and all kinds of innovation in the business community. What I find significant about (for instance) Richard Florida's *The Rise of the Creative Class* is the manner in which he tries to connect the (supposed) autonomy of artists and cultural workers to the work of those involved in the high tech industry.[24] Florida's argument is that more and more workers are becoming freer and freer (and also generating more money) because they are engaged in creative work in a manner that is similar to artists. In his eyes, artists have the maximum creativity, spending their days engaged in self-expression and self-definition. We're lucky then to live at a moment when *all* work becomes akin to being an artist, as we can thus express our creativity at work as well as at play. What Florida and other champions of creativity overlook is, first, that many artists and cultural workers continue to receive far from living wages, and second, that those who are being creative in the tech industries are also receiving salaries that are less than they otherwise might. The (supposed) joys of being able to be creative seems to blind these workers to the fact that their employers are still making a surplus off of their labour. But even beyond this, I can't help but be suspicious of the very idea of creativity. It seems to do little real analytic work in comparison to its ideological function, which can range from expressions of pleasure or approval, to covering up the exploitation and the extraction of surplus through the narrative that we are all artists now, and so have reached whatever self-fulfillment we might expect from society. Creativity is far from a coherent concept, though we often enough take it to be so. In my reading of Florida's work, creativity has multiple, often contradictory definitions.[25] It is at times an innate quality of the human everyone possesses; at other times, this quality is shared unequally, such that only some will ever be creative (and this is determined genetically); sometimes it is a cultural characteristic (some cultures being more creative than others), other times it is associated with certain kinds of work; frequently it is tied simply to innovation, and even more specifically, to innovations in technology.

For artists and cultural producers, the sudden importance of creative labour – and associated concepts, such as creative cities – might make it seem as if it their own work has finally assumed the social importance they always imagined for it. To whatever degree, in an effort to develop the immaterial and affective aspects of their economies in the new century, cities, regions and countries around the world have created programs to support and encourage culture. Instead of being a drain on economies, the arts and culture sector is now seen as a having a positive fiscal impact on the economy. So one might think: even if creativity is a specious concept, what could be wrong with taking advantage of creative discourses that help generate more money for museums, increase grants for artists, expand government sponsorship of festivals, and so on?

I don't see it this way. The use of the concept of creativity to render non-cultural activities as having the same freedom as artists' work functions to transform a romantic fiction of the latter into a way of affirming the permanence of labour under capitalism – which now becomes okay because it is creative, and so unalienated, too! It also undermines the relative autonomy of arts and culture – an autonomy (however questionable, however problematic at a theoretical level) that enabled and supported a critical vantage point on the social and political. Yúdice writes that "the role of culture has expanded in an unprecedented way into the political and economic at the same time that conventional notions of culture largely have been emptied out."[26] If culture has become a protagonist, it is only through an emptying out of any critical notion of the arts and culture. It may well be that culture is the ultimate commodity. The profit margins on cultural goods can be huge, and it seems to be as necessary to our daily lives as food and water. But this of course is a further problem of our moment as opposed to anything like a solution – a collapse of art and life that is perverse in ways well beyond the trauma of the rise of mass culture that concerned Peter Bürger in his meditations on the fate of the avant garde. And though one element of capital might champion creative culture and creative cities, I suspect that even so it is funding for arts and culture that will be most deeply impacted by austerity measures around the globe. As the Dutch example you point to makes evident, when money is in short supply, whether due to a lack in taxes coming in (in the case of states) or a drop in consumer spending, there is a quick turn to 'vulgar' analyses of what is most socially significant or important. Culture and the arts usually don't cut it – and I should add, this vulgar analysis doesn't always need fiscal shortfalls to animate states or companies to reduce their support.

We're in an interregnum. We continue to operate with older ideas of the critical capacities of art and culture. We've challenged from multiple perspectives some of the problems and limits of a critical autonomy that comes only through a separation from life. Yet given the examples of an art integrated with life, whether this is Bourriaud's aesthetics or the world of immaterial labour named in Florida's use of creativity, we can't help but want to return to an older configuration of the politics of the aesthetic, unless we decide to abandon the equation of art and politics entirely. This is something that, for instance, Gerald Raunig seems to do in *Art and Revolution*, where he re-narrates the avant garde as a series of "transitions, overlaps and concatenations of art and revolution [that] become possible for a limited time, but without synthesis and identification."[27] But to say we're in an interregnum is far from saying that things are hopeless, or that art is compromised and can generate no political insight or action.

Surveying the landscape of contemporary art, Rasmussen

offers the following account of where aesthetics stands in relation to politics at the present time:

> traditional forms of intellectual and aesthetic opposition no longer seem to be at all available. Visual images as well as words and music appear to lack their former alienating effect and are rarely antagonistic towards the prevailing order. Wherever we direct our gaze, it is the complicity of the art institution with the established power that is most conspicuous. The speculation economy of neoliberal capitalism pumped huge sums of money into the art market after 1989, with the result that art today is closely tied to the transnational circulation of capital. At the same time national governments, provinces and cities use art as a marketing instrument in the febrile competition for manpower, investments and tourists. These developments towards an ever-closer link between art and capital, and between art and the ruling order, are undoubtedly the predominant tendency when it comes to contemporary art.[28]

This passage can be read as listing a series of failures – as the ever-greater deterioration of the critical capacities of art and culture. But it can also be read as a blunt, non-moralizing description of where we are, whether we like it or not; that is, as an outline of the challenging circumstances in which we find ourselves. Is it a complete list? No. However, by not naming those critical capacities and possibilities that do exist it is pessimistic and one-sided in the extreme. And there is a developmental narrative suggested that is often present when we paint pictures of where we find ourselves, one that suggests that an open door that once existed is not only being closed but written out of the picture. Better instead to understand that every moment has its crises and problems. Our challenge as scholars is to understand these so that we might do our part in making sure that what appears on the other side of the interregnum is a reality we would want to live in rather than merely endure.

Notes

Art World as Zombie Culture: Excellence, Exodus and Ideology

1.   Marc Mayer interviewed by Jelena Adzic, "Diaspora Art," *The National*, CBC television, February 2, 2010.

2.   Slavoj Žižek, *First as Tragedy, Then as Farce* (London: Verso, 2009) 5.

3.   The website www.excellenceatthenationalgallery.blogspot .com/ is headed with the statement: "We are a growing collective of cultural producers from Canada and abroad concerned with the outrageous and blatantly anachronistic policy of exclusion recently asserted by the Director of the National Gallery of Canada, Marc Mayer, during an interview aired as part of a segment on diaspora art on CBC's 'The National' on February 2, 2010." The website begins with the document "An Open Letter to Marc Mayer, Director, National Gallery of Canada" and is followed by a list of signatories and some of the letters to the editor that subsequently appeared in the *Ottawa Citizen*.

4.   See http://www.excellenceatthenationalgallery.blogspot. com/.

5.   Ernesto Laclau and Chantal Mouffe, *Hegemony and Socialist Strategy: Towards a Radical Democratic Politics* (London: Verso, 1985).

6.   On this see Slavoj Žižek, "Tolerance as an Ideological Category," *Critical Inquiry* #34 (Summer 2008) 660-82.

7.   Žižek, *First as Tragedy, Then as Farce*, 22.

8.   Žižek, *First as Tragedy, Then as Farce*, 22.

9.   See Jacques Rancière, *On the Shores of Politics* (London: Verso, [1992] 2007) 31.

10.   Brian Holmes, "Transparency and Exodus: Political Process in the Mediated Democracies," in *Unleashing the Collective Phantoms: Essays in Reverse Imagineering* (Brooklyn:

Autonomedia, 2008) 181.

11. On this theme, see Gerald Raunig, "On the Breach," *Artforum* (May 2008) 341-343, and Raunig, "Modifying the Grammar: Paolo Virno's Works on Virtuosity and Exodus," *Artforum* (January 2008) 245-250.

12. Holmes, "Transparency and Exodus: Political Process in the Mediated Democracies," 186.

13. Holmes, "Transparency and Exodus: Political Process in the Mediated Democracies," 178.

14. "At a larger scale we can see that the tremendous ambivalence of the 1990s – by which I mean the violent deterritorialization of the capitalist globalization process, paralleled by the extraordinary freedom of communicational experimentation, the emergence all over the world of new social movements in the wake of the Zapatistas, and the first attempts at coordinated global struggles – has now given rise to exactly what the philosophical generation of the 1970s taught us to recognize and to flee: the 'dialectical' return of the same, through the clash of seeming opposites." Holmes, "Emancipation," in *Unleashing the Collective Phantoms*, 152.

15. Ricrado Balli of the Association of Autonomous Astronauts cited in Holmes, "Unleashing the Collective Phantoms," in *Unleashing the Collective Phantoms*, 23. See also Ewen Chardronnet, *Quitter la gravité* (Nîmes: L'éclat, 2001).

16. Boris Karloff, "Resisting Zombie Culture," talk delivered at Public Netbase, Vienna, available at http://www.uncarved.org/turb/articles/karloff.html.

17. Slavoj Žižek, "The Return to Hegel," lecture delivered at the European Graduate School, March 1, 2010, available at http://www.youtube.com/watch?v=aR3vfHuOW38.

18. Janet Wolff, "The Ideology of Autonomous Art," in Richard Leppert and Susan McClary, eds. *Music and Society: The Politics of Composition, Performance and Reception*

(Cambridge: Cambridge University Press, 1987) 1-12.

19. See for instance, Gerald Raunig, *Art and Revolution: Transversal Activism in the Long Twentieth Century*, trans. Aileen Derieg (Los Angeles: Semiotext(e), 2007) and Gavin Grindon, "Surrealism, Dada, and the Refusal of Work: Autonomy, Activism, and Social Participation in the Radical Avant-Garde," *Oxford Art Journal* 34:1 (2011) 79-96. See also Peter Bürger, *Theory of the Avant-Garde*, trans. Michael Shaw (Minneapolis: University of Minnesota Press, [1974], 1984).

20. Bill Readings, *The University in Ruins* (Cambridge: Harvard University Press, 1996).

21. See Janet Wolff, "Against Sociological Imperialism: The Limits of Sociology in the Aesthetic Sphere," in Ronald W. Neperud, ed. *Context, Content, and Community in Art Education* (New York: The Teachers College Press, 1995) 128-140.

22. A similar argument is put forward from a postcolonial perspective by Arif Dirlik in "Our Ways of Knowing: Globalization – The End of Universalism?" in Petra Rethmann, Imre Szeman, and William D. Coleman, eds. *Cultural Autonomy: Frictions and Connections* (Vancouver: UBC Press, 2010) 28-48.

23. See Slavoj Žižek, *On Belief* (London: Routledge, 2001).

Culture and the Communist Turn

1. Michael Hardt and Antonio Negri, "Arabs Are Democracy's New Pioneers," *Interactivist Info Exchange* (February 25, 2011), available at http://interactivist.autonomedia.org /node/14284.

2. See for instance, Anne Alexander, "The Gravedigger of Dictatorship," *Socialist Review* (March 2011), available at http://www.socialistreview.org.uk/article.php?articlenumbe r=11580.

3. The third annual conference of the Critical Social Research

Collaborative, "Varieties of Socialism, Varieties of Approaches," was held at Carleton University, Ottawa, on Saturday March 5, 2011.

4. Presentations from the 2010 Creative Time Summit, titled "Revolutions in Public Practice," can be viewed online at: http://creativetime.org/programs/archive/2010/summit/swf.html.

5. Maude Barlow and Tony Clark, *Global Showdown: How the New Activists Are Fighting Global Corporate Rule* (Toronto: Stoddart, 2001).

6. George Yúdice, *The Expediency of Culture: Uses of Culture in the Global Era* (Durham: Duke University Press, 2003).

7. Chris Harman, *Zombie Capitalism: Global Resistance and the Relevance of Marx* (London: Bookmarks Publications, 2009) 201.

8. Harman, *Zombie Capitalism*, 223.

9. Harman, *Zombie Capitalism*, 331. See Ernesto Laclau and Chantal Mouffe, *Hegemony and Socialist Strategy: Towards a Radical Democratic Politics* (London: Verso, 1985); Michael Hardt and Antonio Negri, *Empire* (Cambridge: Harvard University Press, 2000).

10. Harman, *Zombie Capitalism*, 332.

11. Harman, *Zombie Capitalism*, 336.

12. István Mészáros, *The Challenge and Burden of Historical Time: Socialism in the Twenty-First Century* (New York: Monthly Review Press, 2008) 78.

13. István Mészáros, *The Challenge and Burden of Historical Time*, 77.

14. Karl Heinz Roth, "Global Crisis – Global Proletarianization – Counter-perspectives," *Wildcat* (December 2008), available at http://www.wildcat-www.de/en/actual/e068roth_crisis.html.

15. We should of course question this idea of developed and undeveloped. As Eduardo Galeano so aptly put it about

Latin America: "In these lands we are not experiencing the primitive infancy of capitalism but its vicious senility. Underdevelopment isn't a stage of development, but its consequence." Eduardo Galeano, *Open Veins: Latin America: Five Centuries of the Pillage of a Continent* (New York: Monthly Review Press, 1973) 307.

16. Doug Henwood, "I am a Fighting Atheist: Interview with Slavoj Žižek," *Bad Subjects* #59 (February 2002), available at http://criticaltheory-download-ebooks.blogspot.com/2011/02/i-am-fighting-atheist-interview-with.html.

17. Žižek in Henwood, "I am a Fighting Atheist: Interview with Slavoj Žižek."

18. Slavoj Žižek, *Iraq: The Borrowed Kettle* (London: Verso, 2004) 98.

19. Alain Badiou, *Ethics: An Essay on the Understanding of Human Evil*, trans. Peter Hallward (London: Verso, 1993).

20. See Slavoj Žižek, *In Defense of Lost Causes* (London: Verso, 2008) 182.

21. Žižek, *In Defense of Lost Causes*, 183.

22. Pierre Bourdieu, *Distinction: A Social Critique of the Judgement of Taste*, trans. Richard Nice (Cambridge: Harvard University Press, [1979] 1984).

23. The discussion group Markets included Anton Vidokle, J. Morgan Puett, Surasi Kusolwong, Superflex, and Julia Bryan-Wilson. Food included Amy Franceschini, Agnes Denes, InCUBATE, F.E.A.S.T and Claire Pentecost; Schools involved Jakob Jakobsen, The Bruce High Quality Foundation, Learning Site, and Saskia Bos; Governments included Laura Kurgan, Chen Chien-Jen, Oliver Ressler, PLATFORM and Aaron Levy; Institutions was comprised of Thomas Keenan, Danielle Abrams, Otabenga Jones & Associates, W.A.G.E. and Andrea Fraser; Plausible Art Worlds included Chto Delat, Eating in Public, The International Errorist, Scott Rigby and Stephen Wright. This

conference also included presentations by Anne Pasternak, Gridthiya Gaweewong, Sofia Hernández Chong Cuy, Rick Lowe, Trevor Paglen, Shaun Gladwell, Dinh Q. Lê, Regina Tosé Galindo, Phil Collins, Eyal Weizman, Laurie Jo Reynolds, Chris Martinez, Claire Doherty, Bisi Silva, Kickstarter, Basekamp, Stephen Wright, Tidad Zolghadr, and keynote speaker Wendell Pierce.

24.   Peter Bürger, *Theory of the Avant-Garde,* trans. Michael Shaw (Minneapolis: University of Minnesota Press, [1974] 1984).

25.   This could be said of three recent contributions to the literature on social practice: Grant H. Kester, *The One and the Many: Contemporary Collaborative Art in a Global Context* (Durham: Duke University Press, 2011), Claire Bishop, *Artificial Hells: Participatory Art and the Politics of Spectatorship* (London: Verso, 2012), and Nato Thompson, ed. *Living as Form: Socially Engaged Art from 1991-2011* (Cambridge: The MIT Press, 2012).

Alterglobal Allegory: Condé and Beveridge Against the Commodification of Water

1.   Declan McGonagle, "Reflections on the Politics of Practice and the Art of Condé and Beveridge," in Bruce Barber, ed. *Condé and Beveridge: Class Works* (Halifax/Kingston: The Press of the Nova Scotia College of Art and Design/Agnes Etherington Art Centre, 2008) 32.

2.   See for example Nicolas Bourriaud, *Relational Aesthetics,* trans. Simon Pleasance et al. (Paris: Les presses du réel, [1998] 2002).

3.   McGonagle, "Reflections on the Politics of Practice and the Art of Condé and Beveridge," 32.

4.   Diana Nemiroff, "Maybe It's Only Politics: Carole Condé and Karl Beveridge," *Vanguard* 11:8-9 (October/November 1982) 8, 11.

5.   Martha Fleming, "The Production of Meaning: Karl

Beveridge and Carole Condé," Special Issue of *Open Letter* edited by Bruce Barber, *Open Letter* #5-6 (Summer-Fall 1983)147-8.

6. See, respectively, Linda Hutcheon, *Splitting Images* (Toronto: Oxford University Press, 1991); Suzanne Lacy, ed. *Mapping the Terrain: New Genre Public Art* (Seattle: Bay Press, 1995); Grant Kester, *Conversation Pieces: Community + Communication in Modern Art* (Berkeley: University of California Press, 2004). For an example of the innocuous ascription of Condé and Beveridge's work to a progressive liberal "new genre public art," see Martha Langford, "Workers in Progress: The Art of Condé and Beveridge," *Border Crossings* (2006) 98-103.

7. Fleming, "The Production of Meaning," 140.

8. Wolfgang Zinggl, "From the Object to the Concrete Intervention," in Zinggl, ed. *WochenKlausur: Sociopolitical Activism in Art* (Vienna: Springer, 2001) 11.

9. Fleming, "The Production of Meaning," 145.

10. Andrea Fraser, "How Has Art Changed?" *Frieze* #94 (October 2005), available at http://www.frieze.com /issue/article/how_has_art_changed/.

11. Chto Delat, "A Declaration on Politics, Knowledge and Art," available at http://www.chtodelat.org/index.php?option= com_content&task=view&id=494&Item.

12. Brian Holmes, "Extradisciplinary Investigations: For a New Critique of Institutions," in *Escape the Overcode: Activist Art in the Control Society* (Eindhoven: Van Abbemuseum, 2010) 105-6. See also Gerald Raunig, *Art and Revolution: Transversal Activism in the Long Twentieth Century*, trans. Aileen Derieg (Los Angeles: Semiotext(e), 2007).

13. Pascal Gielen and Sonja Lavaert, "The Dismeasure of Art: An Interview with Paolo Virno," *Open* #17 (2009), available at http://www.skor.nl/article-4178-en.html.

14. On this subject, see Maude Barlow and Tony Clark, *Blue*

Gold: The Battle Against Corporate Theft of the World's Water (London: Earthscan Publications, 2002).

15. Benjamin writes that in German baroque drama, or plays of sorrow, the content deals with historical life interpreted through the vicissitudes of court life. The Prince is the representative of history and his ultimate authority compels either fear or pity. No real satisfaction, Benjamin argues, can be had in the tyrant's fall, for his fate is held to be synonymous with that of the people. Rather like Christ, royalty suffers in the name of mankind. An allegory fitting of Benjamin's *Trauerspiel* would be the underwater conference held on October 17 of 2009 – only a few weeks before the climate summit in Copenhagen – by Mohamed Nasheed, the President of the Island nations of the Maldives. If Copenhagen fails, the President said, "we are all going to die." For more on the Maldives case in relation to global warming and rising sea levels, see Mark Lynas, *High Tide: News from a Warming World* (London: HarperCollins, 2004). See also Walter Benjamin, *The Origin of German Tragic Drama*, trans. John Osborne (London: Verso, [1977] 1990) 65.

16. Tuer writes, for example, that *The Fall of Water* is about class struggle "after the end of revolution," with the "disappearance of the proletariat from an image economy," and becoming "the mythic expression of the multitude's struggle for its very existence." Dot Tuer, "The Politics of Recognition," in *Condé and Beveridge: Class Works*, 51-57. See also Michael Hardt and Antonio Negri, *Empire* (Cambridge: Harvard University Press, 2000) and Paolo Virno, *A Grammar of the Multitude: For an Analysis of Contemporary Forms of Life* (New York: Semiotext(e), 2004).

17. Email correspondence with Carole Condé and Karl Beveridge, May 24, 2010.

By Any Means Necessary: From the Revolutionary Art of Emory Douglas to the Art Activism of Jackie Sumell

1.   Slavoj Žižek, "Class Struggle or Postmodernism? Yes, Please!" in Judith Butler, Ernesto Laclau and Slavoj Žižek, *Contingency, Hegemony, Universality: Contemporary Dialogues on the Left* (London: Verso, 2000) 90-135.

2.   Slavoj Žižek, "Tolerance as an Ideological Category," *Critical Inquiry* #34 (Summer 2008) 660-82.

3.   Slavoj Žižek, *Iraq: The Borrowed Kettle* (London: Verso, 2004) 98.

4.   Alain Badiou, *The Meaning of Sarkozy*, trans. David Fernbach (London: Verso, [2007] 2008) 113.

5.   This platform was written by Party co-founders Bobby Seale and Huey Newton on October 22, 1966. What distinguished the Panthers from other black civil rights groups was its emphasis on the right to self-defense, and, following Malcolm X's break with the Nation of Islam, its position against the xenophobia of black nationalists. Making use of a California law that allowed citizens to carry unloaded rifles in public, Seale and Newton created one of the key elements in the original Panther image, which included black leather jackets, black slacks, shiny shoes and berets – a uniform inspired by a viewing of a film about the French resistance. The first government action against the Panthers was a repeal of the gun law. See Stephen Shames, *The Black Panthers: Photographs by Stephen Shames* (New York: Aperture, 2006).

6.   Mike Kelley cited in Sylvère Lotringer, "Consumed by Myths," in *Premises: Invested Spaces in Visual Arts, Architecture & Design from France: 1958-1998* (New York: Guggenheim Museum, 1998) 33.

7.   Sam Durant, ed. *Black Panther: The Revolutionary Art of Emory Douglas* (New York: Rizzoli, 2007).

8.   Colette Gaiter, "What Revolution Looks Like: The Work of

Black Panther Artist Emory Douglas," in Durant, ed. *Black Panther*, 95.

9. Greg Jung Morozumi, "Emory Douglas and the Third World Cultural Revolution," in Durant, ed. *Black Panther*, 136.

10. See Erika Doss, "'Revolutionary Art Is a Tool for Liberation': Emory Douglas and Protest Aesthetics at the *Black Panther*," in Kathleen Cleaver and George Katsiaficas, eds. *Liberation, Imagination, and the Black Panther Party: A New Look at the Panthers and their Legacy* (New York: Routledge, 2001) 175-87. For a more even treatment of the subject of masculinism in the BPP, see Matthew W. Hughey, "Black Aesthetics and Panther Rhetoric: A Critical Decoding of Black Masculinity in *The Black Panther*," *Critical Inquiry* 35:1 (2009) 29-56.

11. Homi K. Bhabha cited in Rosalyn Deutsche, "Surprising Geography," *Annals of the Association of American Geographers* 85:1 (1995) 172.

12. See Angela Davis, "How Does Change Happen?" lecture delivered at the University of California at Davis, October 10, 2006, available at http://www.youtube.com/watch?v=Pc6RHtEbi0A.

13. Kathleen Cleaver, "Women, Power and Revolution," in Cleaver and Katsiaficas, eds. *Liberation, Imagination, and the Black Panther Party*, 124.

14. Michael Schudson, "Cultural Studies and the Social Construction of 'Social Construction': Notes on 'Teddy Bear Patriarchy'," in Elizabeth Long, ed. *From Sociology to Cultural Studies: New Perspectives* (Oxford: Blackwell, 1997) 380.

15. Schudson, "Cultural Studies and the Social Construction of 'Social Construction'," 389.

16. Slavoj Žižek, "A Plea for 'Eurocentrism'," in Žižek, *The Universal Exception: Selected Writings, Volume Two*, eds. Rex

Butler and Scott Stephens (London: Continuum, 2006) 187.

17. Angela Davis and Bettina Aptheker in Angela Davis and other political prisoners, *If They Come in the Morning* (New York: Signet, 1971) xiii.

18. Davis, "Political Prisoners, Prisons and Black Liberation," in Davis, *If They Come in the Morning*, 30-1.

19. For a detailed analysis of this case, see Scott Fleming, "Lockdown at Angola: The Case of the Angola 3," in Cleaver and Katsiaficas, eds. *Liberation, Imagination, and the Black Panther Party*, 229-36. See also www.angola3.org.

20. I first saw Sumell's CAD video at the 2008 *Dissident Art* exhibition organized by the Montreal Art + Anarchie collective. See www.artdissidentart.com. The website for Sumell's series of projects is www.hermanshouse.org. I interviewed Sumell in Montreal on February 10, 2010, after a lecture she gave that was sponsored by the Leonard & Bina Ellen Gallery, Concordia University, and the Goethe Institute, Montreal.

21. Brian Holmes, "Risk of the New Vanguards," contribution to issue number 17 of Chto Delat, *What Is to Be Done? Debates on the Avant-Garde* (2009), available at http://www.chtod elat.org/images/pdfs/17_vanguard.pdf.

22. Noam Chomsky, *Class Warfare: Noam Chomsky Interviewed by David Barsamian* (Vancouver: New Star Books, 1997) 31.

Afterthoughts on Engaged Art Practice: ATSA and the State of Emergency

1. Clement Greenberg, "Avant-Garde and Kitsch," in *Art and Culture: Critical Essays* (Boston: Beacon Press, 1961) 5.

2. See Mary Jane Jacob, Michael Brenson, and Eva M. Olson, *Culture in Action: A Public Art Program of Sculpture Chicago* (Seattle: Bay Press, 1995); Suzanne Lacy, ed. *Mapping the Terrain: New Genre Public Art* (Seattle: Bay Press, 1995); Miwon Kwon, *One Place after Another: Site-Specific Art and*

Locational Identity (Cambridge: MIT Press, 2002); Claire Bishop, "Antagonism and Relational Aesthetics," *October* #110 (Fall 2004) 51-79; Grant H. Kester, *Conversation Pieces: Community and Communication in Modern Art* (Berkeley: University of California Press, 2004); Bruce Barber, *Performance, [Performance] and Performers, Volume 2*, ed. Marc James Léger (Toronto: YYZBOOKS, 2007).

3. See Brian Holmes, "Extradisciplinary Investigations: Towards a New Critique of Institutions," in *Escape the Overcode: Activist Art in the Control Society* (Eindhoven: Van Abbemuseum, 2009) 98-123. Similar assertions are made by Gene Ray and Gregory Sholette in "Introduction: Whither Tactical Media?" *Third Text* 22:5 (September 2008) 519–24.

4. Martha Rosler, "In, Around, and Afterthoughts (On Documentary Photography)," in *Martha Rosler: 3 Works* (Halifax: Press of the Nova Scotia College of Art and Design, 1981) 59-87.

5. Wolfgang Zinggl, "From the Object to the Concrete Intervention," in *WochenKlausur: Sociopolitical Activism in Art*, ed. Zinggl (Vienna: Springer, 2001) 11.

6. Sentence number eighteen in Barber's 1998 "Sentences on Littoral Art" reads: "Littoralist artists acknowledge their debt to history and respond positively to successful models presented by the historical avant-gardes and neo-avant-gardes of the more recent past." See http://www.bruce-barber.ca/novelsquat/index2.html.

7. Nato Thompson, "Trespassing Relevance," in *The Interventionists: Users' Manual for the Creative Disruption of Everyday Life*, ed. Thompson and Gregory Sholette (Cambridge: MIT Press, 2004) 21-2.

8. Chto Delat, "A Declaration on Politics, Knowledge and Art," available at http://www.chtodelat.org/index.php?option=com_content&task=view&id=494&Item.

9. See David Graeber, "Some Notes on 'Activist Culture'," in

Direct Action: An Ethnography (Oakland: AK Press, 2009) 239-62. The dilemma in the antinomy of alienation and oppression, as Graeber states it, are the discrepancies in the moral weight of struggle. On this I agree with Slavoj Žižek that identity struggles often transform politico-economic struggles into pseudo-psychoanalytic dramas of the subject who is intolerant of the Other and unable to confront the stranger within. Capitalism no longer stands in the way of counter-cultural practices, especially since no individual disposition can be made the object of a universal exemplar-iness. On the other hand, capitalism does actively thwart socialist and revolutionary organization, especially where it is effective. Here, the more utopian strains in the movement have been somewhat complacent to the extent that people have come to believe that community gardens and alter-native lifestyles are in some way a threat to the status quo. On this, see Marc James Léger, "Welcome to the Cultural Goodwill Revolution: On Class Composition in the Age of Classless Struggle," *Journal of Aesthetics and Protest #7* (2009), available oat http://joaap.org/7/leger.html.

10. ATSA's first project was a response to the 1997 headline that Canadian banks had made more than seven billion dollars in record profits, whereas the local shelter and service provider, *La Maison du Père*, needed more than one hundred pairs of socks for its homeless clients. A sculptural instal-lation of ovens containing warm socks was set up by the newly formed and unknown ATSA on the Place des Arts esplanade in front of the Musée d'art contemporain de Montréal. The former director of the museum, Marcel Brisebois, allowed the sculpture to be brought inside the museum's lobby, giving ATSA an unexpected "foot in the door" of the art world. Two years later, the City of Montreal declined to allow the event to take place on Place Émilie-Gamelin, often frequented by junkies, and so ATSA collabo-

rated with a nearby private partner. In 2000 *EU* was refused by both the Canadian Armed Forces and the City of Montreal, and an impromptu event was organized on the corner of Clark Street and Sainte-Catherine. Since 2002, the Tremblay administration became a long-term partner, allowing *EU* to take on the dimensions it is now known for with its three white army-size tents and stage. By 2006 it garnered routine media coverage and the group has been approached by the cities of Calgary, Vancouver, and Toronto to set up similar events in their jurisdictions.

11. See the 2009 *EU* page on ATSA's web site: http://atsa. qc.ca/projs/eu09/uk/motatsa.html.

12. See Sonia Pelletier, "An Encounter with ATSA," in *ATSA: Quand l'art passe à l'action (When Art Takes Action)* (Montreal: Action Terroriste Socialement Acceptable, 2008) 11.

13. See Louis Jacob, "On Art and Wandering: *État d'Urgence* at Place Émilie-Gamelin," in *ATSA: Quand l'art passe à l'action*, 59.

14. Homelessness is also often thought of as a timeless condition in relation to which there should be room in society for people to simply fall out of normal sociality. These kinds of arguments support neoliberal policies that seek to disinvest in public services. Homelessness, minimally, can be attributed not only to individual circumstances like drug addiction and mental illness, but to economic processes, state planning, and social conflict. The urban, in this regard, becomes a site for the reproduction of capitalist social relations, transforming space into the private ownership of real estate, understood as a commodity that is traded for the purposes of profiteering. State planning facilitates this process by regulating the conflicts that arise and legitimizing capitalist exchange as democratic. Under neoliberal policy, public resources are used to subsidize urban development, for example, through

private-public partnerships and by withdrawing social services. The symptom of this privatization of land use, according to Rosalyn Deutsche, is the creation of pseudo-public spaces and pseudo-historic districts, and the eviction of residents who can no longer afford to live in gentrified neighborhoods. As public resources are privatized and manufacturing is moved offshore, employment becomes scarce, leading to a new, precarious economy based on nonproductive, service-sector employment. See Deutsche, "Alternative Space," in Brian Wallis, ed. *If You Lived Here: The City in Art, Theory, and Social Space* (Seattle: Bay Press, 1991) 44-65.

15. See Michael Sorkin, ed. *Variations on a Theme Park: The New American City and the End of Public Space* (New York: Hill and Wang, 1992).

16. Although I did not manage to see it, the works on show included a miniature cardboard *favela* by the Brazilian artist Sérgio Cezar. Annie Roy told reporters that Cezar, whom she met at the Havana Bienal, had been invited "to remind people that [homelessness] is not just a local issue but a global one." Michael-Oliver Harding, "Favela Modeling," *Montreal Mirror* (November 26-December 2, 2009) 10.

17. The involvement of children in the serving of Le Banquet cochon, a spectacular five-course meal, is appropriate, especially considering that children in Canada account for roughly 40 percent of food bank users. Despite government promises to eliminate child poverty, it actually increased in the mid-1990s and 2000s. The use of food banks in Canada has increased by roughly 20 percent over the last two years. See Ashifa Kassan, "Still Below the Poverty Line, 20 Years Later," *rabble.ca* (December 7, 2009), available at http://www.rabble.ca/columnists/2009/12/still-below-the-poverty-line.

18. Slavoj Žižek, "Post-Wall," *London Review of Books* (November

19, 2009), available at http://www.lrb.co.uk/v31/n22/slavoj-zizek/post-wall.

19. See Slavoj Žižek, "First as Tragedy, Then as Farce," lecture delivered at Cooper Union, October 14, 2009, available at http://www.youtube.com/watch?v=tW1NIB9MmSo.

20. Martha Rosler, "Fragments of a Metropolitan Viewpoint," in Wallis, ed. *If You Lived Here*, 34.

21. See especially, Judith Butler, Ernesto Laclau, and Slavoj Žižek, *Contingency, Hegemony, Universality: Contemporary Dialogues on the Left* (London: Verso, 2000).

22. See Slavoj Žižek, *The Universal Exception: Selected Writings, Volume 2,* ed. Rex Butler and Scott Stephens (London: Continuum, 2006).

23. See for example, Paolo Virno, *A Grammar of the Multitude: For an Analysis of Contemporary Forms of Life* (New York: Semiotext(e), 2004).

24. Hal Foster, "Precarious," *Artforum* (December 2009), available at http://findarticles.com/p/articles/mi_m0268/is_4_48/ai_n56388185/.

25. Hal Foster, "Precarious."

26. Gerald Raunig, "The Monster Precariat," *Translate* (2007), available at http://translate.eipcp.net/strands/02/raunig-strands02en#redir.

27. Guy Sioui Durand addresses such conflicts when he suggests that ATSA's work combines a macro-political aesthetic that complements alter-protesting along with micro-political "citizen" interventions. See Durand, "The Aesthetic of Outrage: Action Terroriste Socialement Acceptable (ATSA) 1997–2007," in *ATSA: Quand l'art passe à l'action*, 21.

28. BAVO, "Introduction: Cultural Activism Today. The Art of Over-Identification," in BAVO, ed. *Cultural Activism Today: The Art of Over-Identification* (Rotterdam: Episode, 2007) 7.

29. BAVO, "Introduction: Cultural Activism Today. The Art of Over-Identification," 7. See also BAVO, "The Spectre of the Avant-Garde: Contemporary Reassertions of the Programme of Subversion in Cultural Production," *Andere Sinema* #176 (2006) 24-41.

30. The last time I heard this was on the occasion of former US President George W. Bush's visit to Montreal on October 22, 2009, to deliver a talk to the local Chamber of Commerce. Among the companies represented at the talk was SNC Lavalin, the corporate sponsor of the 1999 *État d'Urgence*. The company allowed ATSA to organize the *EU* on its privately owned plaza after the Bourque administration had turned down the requested Place Émilie-Gamelin.

31. See Murray Dobbin, "Harper Pledges to Sabotage Climate Change Agenda at G20," *rabble.ca* (December 9, 2009), available at http://www.rabble.ca/blogs/bloggers/murray-dobbin/2009/12/harper-pledges-sabotage-climate-change-agenda-g20.

The Non-Productive Role of the Artist: The Creative Industries in Canada

1. Kirsty Robertson, "Crude Culture: The Creative Industries in Canada," *Fuse Magazine* (April 2008) 12-21.

2. Robertson, "Crude Culture," 21. I agree with Robertson that this is odd since the primary purpose of the Summit was clearly oriented toward the commercial promotion of Canadian visual art.

3. Jim Stanford, "Corporate Canada's Enemy Lurks Within," *rabble.ca* (June 8, 2009), available at http://www.rabble.ca/columnists/2009/06/corporate-canada-enemy-work-within. As a point of fact, according to Maude Barlow and Tony Clark, Canadians own a smaller portion of their productive wealth than any other industrialized country. See Barlow and Clark, *Global Showdown: How the New*

Activists are Fighting Global Corporate Rule (Toronto: Stoddart, 2001) and Jim Stanford, *Economics for Everyone: A Short Guide to the Economics of Capitalism* (Halifax: Fernwood Publishing, 2008).

4. Henri Lefebvre, *De L'État, Volume I: L'État dans le monde moderne* (Paris: 10/18 - Union Générale d'Éditions, 1976).

5. David Morley and Kevin Robins, "Spaces of Identity: Communications Technologies and the Reconfiguration of Europe," *Screen* #30 (1989) 10-34.

6. Bill Readings, *The University in Ruins* (Cambridge: Harvard University Press, 1996). See also Slavoj Žižek, "Multiculturalism, or, the Cultural Logic of Multinational Capitalism," in Žižek, *The Universal Exception: Selected Writings, Volume Two*, eds. Rex Butler and Scott Stephens (London: Continuum, 2006) 151-82.

7. Marc James Léger, "The Colonial Copy," paper presented at the Universities Art Association of Canada Annual Conference, 2005, available at http://legermj.type pad.com/blog/2010/12/the-colonial-copy-ends-of-canadian-art-history.html.

8. Alain Badiou interviewed in *Libération* (January 26, 2009), available at http://www.lacan.com/article/?page_id=125.

9. "Leaders' Debate: The Arts," *National Post* (October 2, 2008), available at http://www.nationalpost.com/news/global-video/index.html.

10. Stephen Harper cited in the Montreal *Mirror* (August 14-20, 2008) 5.

11. David Akin, "Conservatives cancel $4.7M arts travel program," *The Ottawa Citizen* (August 8, 2008), available at http://www.canada.com/ottawacitizen/news/story.html.

12. National Post Editorial Board, "What Counts as 'Culture'?" *National Post* (October 06, 2008).

13. Variant Affinity Group, "Comment," *Variant* (Winter 2008), available   at

http://www.variant.randomstate.org/33texts/1_v33comment 33.html

14. Gregory Sholette, "Disciplining the Avant-Garde: The United States versus The Critical Art Ensemble," *Circa* (Summer 2005) 52.

15. See Richard Sennett and Saskia Sassen, "Guantánamo in Germany," *The Guardian* (August 21, 2007), available at http://www.education/guardian.co.uk/higher/comment/stor y/.

16. See for example, BAVO, "From the Post-Socialist Dutch City to the Retro-Socialist City...and Back! Or, how to subvert today's imperative to re-stage non-capitalist social relations in this so-called post-utopian age?" (2008), available at http://www.bavo.biz/texts/view/15.

17. Maurizio Lazzarato, "Construction of Cultural Labour Market," *Framework* (January 2007), available at http://www.framework.fi/6_2007/locating/artikkelit/lazzarat o.html.

18. Michael Hardt and Antonio Negri, *Empire* (Cambridge: Harvard University Press, 2000) 292.

19. Hardt and Negri, *Empire*, 289-90.

20. Hardt and Negri, *Empire*, 294.

21. These estimates are based on the work of Fred Moseley and Jim Stanford.

22. Richard Florida, *The Rise of the Creative Class: And How It's Transforming Work, Leisure, Community and Everyday Life* (New York: Basic Books, 2002).

23. See Richard Florida, *The Flight of the Creative Class: The New Global Competition for Talent* (New York: HarperCollins, 2005).

24. Angela McRobbie, "'Everyone is Creative': Artists as Pioneers of the New Economy?" in Marc James Léger, ed. *Culture and Contestation in the New Century* (London: Intellect, 2011) 79-92.

25. Aras Ozgun, "Creative Industries: Neo-Liberalism as Mass Deception," in Léger, ed. *Culture and Contestation in the New Century*, 107-23.

26. On this see Slavoj Žižek, *The Puppet and the Dwarf: The Perverse Core of Christianity* (Cambridge: The MIT Press, 2003).

27. Slavoj Žižek, *The Parallax View* (Cambridge: The MIT Press, 2006) 318.

28. Stefan Christoff, "Imagine that, Yoko Ono nails Stephen Harper on Copyright Infringement," *rabble.ca* (April 7, 2011), available at http://www.rabble.ca/news/2011/04/imagine-yoko-ono-nails-stephen-harper-copyright-infringement.

29. "You Tube Pulls Harper Imagine Clip," *CBC News* (April 6, 2011), available at http://www.cbc.ca/news/politics/canadavotes2011/story/2011/04/06/cv-harper-imagine-youtube.html.

Protesting Degree Zero: On Black Bloc Tactics, Culture and Building the Movement

1. The G8, or Group of Eight, is a forum for the member nations of eight of the world's major industrialized economies: France, Germany, Italy, Japan, the U.K., the U.S., the E.U. and Canada. Alterglobalization critics of the G8 and the larger G20 argue that the member states of the two groups are responsible for major global problems that derive from their promotion of neoliberal market ideology. According to the Marxist social scientist David Harvey, neoliberal institutions like the G8 propose that human well-being must be advanced through property rights, free markets and free trade. State interventions must be kept at a minimum and markets should be allowed to bring into effect the benefits of "creative destruction" and of exchange values regardless of attachments to the land or habits of the

heart. Neoliberalism seeks to bring, he writes, "all human interaction into the domain of the market." Harvey adds that unlike the previous welfare state, neoliberal policies have not resulted in higher rates of economic growth but have instead contributed to greater social and class hierarchization. Increasing social inequality, he argues, is structural to the role of neoliberalization. See David Harvey, *A Brief History of Neoliberalism* (Oxford: Oxford University Press, 2005) 2-13.

2.   See Canadian Press, "Suspects arrested after emerging from manhole cover," *CP24* (June 27, 2010), available at http://www.cp24.com/servlet/an/local/CTVNews/20100627/100627_manhole/20100627/?hub=CP24Home.

3.   See Natalie Alcoba, "Banker vs. looter draws a million hits," *The National Post* (July 3, 2010), available at http://www.nationalpost.com/2010/07/03/banker-vs-looter-draws-a-million-hits.

4.   Slavoj Žižek, *Violence: Six Sideways Glances* (New York: Picador, 2008) 1-2.

5.   The "Toronto weekend" involved overlapping meetings of the G8 in Huntsville, Ontario on June 25 and 26, and the G20 in downtown Toronto, June 26 and 27.

6.   Krystalline Kraus, "G8/G20 Communiqué: An activist's guide to the G20 protests, part one," *rabble.ca* (June 22, 2010).

7.   Jesse McLean, "Behind the Black Bloc," *Toronto Star* (Saturday, June 26, 2010).

8.   Judy Rebick, "Toronto Is Burning! Or Is It?" *rabble.ca* (June 27, 2010).

9.   In contrast to Rebick, Klein refused to denounce the "kids in black who smashed windows and burned cop cars," and instead focused on denouncing heads of state. See Naomi Klein, "My City Feels Like a Crime Scene," *rabble.ca* (June 28, 2010). See also Klein, "Naomi Klein to Police: 'Don't play public relations, do your goddamned job!'" *rabble.ca* (June

29, 2010).

10. Rebick, "Toronto Is Burning." In a later statement, Rebick writes: "In the week leading up to the summit, Conservative Cabinet Minister Stockwell Day signaled a particular focus on 'anarchists' for this security crackdown. This simplistic targeting of a long-standing political tradition was further used by police to justify assaults on all demonstrators as well as the round-up of activists by claiming they were hunting for the 'Black Bloc.' This criminalization of activists aimed to silence attempts to address the real issues presented by the G20." See Rebick, "Toronto Call: No more police state tactics," *rabble.ca* (July 1, 2010).

11. Fred Wilson, "Toronto and the G20: Two Worlds, Two Realities," *rabble.ca* (June 28, 2010). A similar denunciation of Black Bloc tactics came from a representative of the Canadian Union of Public Employees (Ontario): "What we have witnessed is nothing short of the abandonment of the rule of law, both by a small group who took part in the protests, and by a massive and heavily armed police force who were charged with overseeing them. (...) And it's a sad day when some of those, who feel powerless to change the direction of their elected leaders, find in that feeling of powerlessness an excuse to break the law and vandalize the property of their fellow citizens and who, in doing so, silence the legitimate voices of so many others whose commitment to protest and dissent is matched by their rejection of violence and vandalism." Cited in Jeff Shantz, "Their Laws – Our Loss," *rabble.ca* (July 15, 2010).

12. Murray Dobbin, "Is this what a police state looks like?" *rabble.ca* (June 30, 2010).

13. On the subject of police provocation and the distinction between bourgeois and proletarian law, see the classic text by Victor Serge, *What Every Radical Should Know About State Repression* (Melbourne: Ocean Press, [1926] 2005).

14. Krystalline Kraus, "G8/G20 Communiqué: Media coverage and public opinion polls," *rabble.ca* (July 3, 2010).

15. See David Graeber, *Direct Action: An Ethnography* (Oakland, CA: AK Press, 2009).

16. Graeber, *Direct Action*, 224.

17. François Dupuis-Déri, *Les Black Blocs: La liberté et l'égalité se manifestent* (Montreal: Lux, 2003) 10.

18. Dupuis-Déri, *Les Black Blocs*, 12.

19. Michael Albert, "On Trashing and Movement Building," (December 1999), available at http://www.3communications.org/on-trashing-and-movement-organizing-by-michael-albert.

20. François Dupuis-Déri, "G20: N'attendez plus les barbares, ils sont là!" *Le Devoir* (June 29, 2010).

21. François Dupuis-Déri, "Penser l'action directe des Black Blocs," *Politix* 17:68 (2004) 80.

22. Dupuis-Déri, "Penser l'action directe des Black Blocs," 94.

23. Žižek, *Violence*, 36.

24. Graeber, *Direct Action*, 254.

25. Raoul Vaneigem, *The Revolution of Everyday Life*, trans. Donald Nicholson-Smith (London: Rebel Press, 2001) 47.

26. Vaneigem, *The Revolution of Everyday Life*, 110.

27. Vaneigem, *The Revolution of Everyday Life*, 260.

28. Vaneigem, *The Revolution of Everyday Life*, 278.

29. Graeber, *Direct Action*, 502.

30. See Historical Film Services, "*The Battle of Orgreave*: Recreating the Climactic Clash of the 1984 Miners' Strike," available at http://www.historicalfilmservices.com/orgreave.htm.

31. Claire Bishop, "The Social Turn," *Artforum* (February 2006) 182. Kester's exact statement, in response to Bishop's article, is as follows: "As delightful as it is to hear yet another disquisition on the glories of *The Battle of Orgreave*, 2001, or *Dogville* (2003), a more complete account of collaborative art

must begin with some measured reflection on the diversity of practices encompassed by that term." Grant Kester, "Another Turn," *Artforum* (May 2006) 22. It should also be mentioned that Bishop has more recently been more appreciative of Deller's project. See Claire Bishop, *Artificial Hells: Participatory Art and the Politics of Spectatorship* (London: Verso, 2012) 30-7.

32. Katie Kitamura, "'Recreating Chaos': Jeremy Deller's *The Battle of Orgreave*," available at http://www.anu.edu.au/hrc /research_platforms/RE-Enactment/Papers/kitamura- katie.pdf.

33. Maria Hlavajova, "Of Training, Imitation and Fiction: A Conversation with Aernout Mik," in Rosi Braidotti, Charles Esche and Maria Hlavajova, eds. *Citizens and Subjects: The Netherlands, for Example* (Zürich: JRP Ringier, 2007) 33.

34. Mik cited in Hlavajova, "Of Training, Imitation and Fiction," 43.

35. Mik cited in Hlavajova, "Of Training, Imitation and Fiction," 36.

36. Oliver Ressler cited in "How Do the Fittest Survive? Interview by Elena Sorokina," *Untitled* #43 (2007), available at http://www.ressler.at/how-do-the-fittest-survive/.

37. Oliver Ressler, statement for *The Fittest Survive* (2006), video, 23 minutes, available at http://www.ressler.at/ the_fittest_survive/.

38. Theodor Adorno, "Transparencies on Film," *New German Critique* #24/25 (Fall/Winter 1981-82) 199-205.

39. Slavoj Žižek, "Lenin's Choice," in *Revolution at the Gates: A Selection of Writings by V.I. Lenin from February to October 1917* (London: Verso, 2002) 227.

40. Mao Zedong cited in John Ellis, "Ideology and Subjectivity," in Stuart Hall et al., eds. *Culture, Media, Language* (London: Hutchinson Education, 1980) 188.

41. See Konrad Becker and Jim Fleming, eds. *Critical Strategies:*

Perspectives on New Cultural Practices (Brooklyn: Autonomedia, 2010).

42. Jim Fleming in *Critical Strategies*, 59.

43. Steve Kurtz in *Critical Strategies*, 25-26.

44. Graeber, *Direct Action*, 299. Gerald Raunig, *A Thousand Machines: A Concise Philosophy of the Machine as Social Movement* (Los Angeles: Semiotext(e), 2010) 16.

45. Raunig, *A Thousand Machines*, 34, 57-8.

46. Raunig, *A Thousand Machines*, 60.

47. Gen Doy, "Women, Class and Photography: The Paris Commune of 1871," in *Seeing and Consciousness: Women, Class and Representation* (Oxford: Berg, 1995) 104.

48. It is perhaps worth mentioning that the leader of our bus to Toronto gave instructions while drinking a Coke brand cola. Similar ironies were played out on the June 25 march by a leftist group that was chanting, "Down with Capitalism! Long Live Socialism!" Every now and then they would reverse the terms: "Down with Socialism! Long Live Capitalism!"

49. Ellis, "Ideology and Subjectivity," 190.

50. See Slavoj Žižek, *Looking Awry: An Introduction to Jacques Lacan through Popular Culture* (Cambridge: The MIT Press, 1991).

The Québec Maple Spring, The Red Square and After

1. See "Droits de scolarité: Marois annule la hausse et une partie de la loi 78," *Le Devoir* (September 20, 2012), available online at http://www.ledevoir.com/politique/quebec/35962 4/droits-de-scolarite-marois-annule-la-hause-mais-maintient-la-bonification-des-prets-et-bourses.

2. Pier Paolo Pasolini, "Civil War," in Jack Hirschman, ed. *In Danger: A Pasolini Anthology* (San Francisco: City Lights Books, 2010) 21.

3. See most notably, Stéphane Hessel's *Time for Outrage!* (New

York and Boston: Twelve, [2010] 2011).

4. For a comparison of democratic versus dialectical materialism, see Bruno Bosteels, *Badiou and Politics* (Durham and London: Duke University Press, 2011).

5. Bosteels, *Badiou and Politics*, 30-1.

6. See "Nous sommes avenir: Manifeste de la CLASSE," July 2012, available at http://issuu.com/asse.solidarite/docs/man ifeste_classe/3. Also available in English as "The CLASSE Manifesto: Share our future," *rabble.ca* (July 12, 2012) http://rabble.ca/blogs/bloggers/campus-notes/2012/07 /classe-manifesto-share-our-future. That the struggle against neoliberal capitalism is understood by the CLASSE in liberal democratic terms, involving a diversity of struggles is confirmed by the press conferences given by spokespersons Gabriel Nadeau-Dubois and Jeanne Reynolds. See for instance "La CLASSE veut se débarasser des néolibéraux," *Le Devoir* (July 13, 2012), available at http://www.ledevoir.com/societe/actualites-en-societe /354508/la-classe-veut-se-debarrasser-des-neoliberaux.

7. See David Harvey, *The Enigma of Capital* (Oxford: Oxford University Press, 2010) 253-9.

8. Gregory Sholette, "Occupology, Swarmology, Whateverology: The city of (dis)order versus the people's archive," *Art Journal* web-only (Winter 2011), available at http:// artjournal.collegeart.org/?p=2395.

9. Situationist International and students of Strasbourg, "On the Poverty of Student Life (1966)," in Ken Knabb, ed. *Situationist International Anthology* (Berkeley: Bureau of Public Secrets, 1981) 321.

10. Bruno Bosteels, *The Actuality of Communism* (London and New York : Verso, 2011) 5-6.

11. Grant Kester, "The Sound of Breaking Glass, Part I: Spontaneity and Consciousness in Revolutionary Theory," *Journal* #30 (December 2011), available at http://www.e-

flux.com/journal/the-sound-of-breaking-glass-part-i-spontaneity-and-consciousness-in-revolutionary-theory/, and "The Sound of Breaking Glass, Part II: Agonism and the Taming of Dissent," *Journal* #31 (January 2012), available at http://www.e-flux.com/journal/the-sound-of-breaking-glass-part-ii-agonism-and-the-taming-of-dissent/.

12. See "Violence et carré rouge: Christine St-Pierre s'excuse," *Radio-Canada.ca* (June 13, 2012), available at http://www.radio-canada.ca/nouvelles/Politique /2012/06/13/002-st-pierre-excuse-carre-violence.shtml.

13. On this subject see Alain Badiou, *The Meaning of Sarkozy*, trans. David Fernbach (London and New York: Verso [2007] 2008).

14. Slavoj Žižek, "Less Than Nothing: Slavoj Žižek in Conversation with Jonathan Derbyshire," lecture at Central Saint Martin's, King's Cross, June 12, 2012, available at http://www.youtube.com/watch?v=hvWkWYHmMxg.

Globalization and the Politics of Culture: An Interview with Imre Szeman

1. Imre Szeman, "Imagining the Future: Globalization, Postmodernism and Criticism," *Frame: Tijdschrift voor Literatuurwetenschap* 19:2 (2006) 16-30; available at http://individual.utoronto.ca/nishashah/Drafts/Szeman.pdf.

2. See Nicolas Bourriaud, *The Radicant* (New York: Lukas & Sternberg, 2009).

3. Peter Bürger, *Theory of the Avant-Garde*, trans. Michael Shaw (Minneapolis: University of Minnesota Press, [1974] 1984).

4. Pierre Bourdieu, *Distinction: A Social Critique of the Judgement of Taste*, trans. Richard Nice (Cambridge: Harvard University Press, [1979] 1984).

5. Jacques Rancière, *The Politics of Aesthetics*, trans. Gabriel Rockhill (London: Continuum, 2004) 19.

6. Nicolas Bourriaud, *Relational Aesthetics*, trans. Simon

Pleasance et al. (Paris: Les presses du réel, [1998] 2002).

7.   Hal Foster, "Chat Rooms," in Claire Bishop, ed. *Participation* (Cambridge: The MIT Press, 2006) 193.

8.   Fredric Jameson, "Transformations of the Image in Postmodernity," in *The Cultural Turn: Selected Writings on the Postmodern, 1983-1998* (New York: Verso, 1998) 135.

9.   Mikkel Bolt Rasmussen, "Scattered (Western Marxist-Style) Remarks about Contemporary Art, Its Contradictions and Difficulties," *Third Text* 25:2 (2011) 199.

10. See Alain Badiou, *The Communist Hypothesis*, trans. David Macey and Steve Corcoran (London: Verso, [2008] 2010).

11. Daniele Archibugi, "Cosmopolitical Democracy," in Archibugi, ed. *Debating Cosmopolitics* (New York: Verso, 2003) 1-15.

12. Timothy Brennan, "Cosmopolitanism and Internationalism," in Daniele Archibugi, ed. *Debating Cosmopolitics*, 42.

13. Immanuel Kant, "Perpetual Peace: A Philosophical Sketch," in *An Answer to the Question: What is Enlightenment?*, trans. H.B. Nisbet (New York: Penguin Books, 2009) 29.

14. Immanuel Kant, "Perpetual Peace," 38.

15. Giorgio Agamben, *The Coming Community*, trans. Michael Hardt (Minneapolis: University of Minnesota Press, [1990] 1993).

16. Imre Szeman, "Marxist Literary Criticism, Then and Now," *Mediations* 24:2 (Spring 2009), available at http://www.mediationsjournal.org/articles/marxist-literary-criticism-then-and-now.

17. Eric Cazdyn and Imre Szeman. *After Globalization* (Oxford: Wiley-Blackwell, 2011).

18. David Harvey, "Feral Capitalism Hits The Streets," *The Bullet* (August 12, 2011).

19. Erik Olin Wright, *Envisioning Real Utopias* (New York: Verso, 2010). *The Power of Community: How Cuba Survived Peak Oil*

(USA, 2006, Faith Morgan).

20. Hal Foster, "Towards a Grammar of Emergency," *New Left Review* #68 (2011) 105.

21. Hal Foster, "Towards a Grammar of Emergency," 114.

22. Raymond Williams, *Marxism and Literature* (Oxford: Oxford University Press, 1977).

23. George Yúdice, *The Expediency of Culture: Uses of Culture in the Global Era*, Durham: Duke University Press, 2003.

24. Florida, Richard. *The Rise of the Creative Class: And How It's Transforming Work, Leisure, Community and Everyday Life* (New York: Basic Books, 2002).

25. Imre Szeman, "Neoliberals Dressed in Black; or, the Traffic in Creativity," *English Studies in Canada* 36:1 (2010) 15-38.

26. Yúdice, *The Expediency of Culture*, 9.

27. Gerald Raunig, *Art and Revolution: Transversal Activism in the Long Twentieth Century*, trans. Aileen Derieg (Los Angeles: Semiotext(e), 2007) 17-8.

28. Rasmussen, "Scattered (Western Marxist-Style) Remarks about Contemporary Art, Its Contradictions and Difficulties," 199.

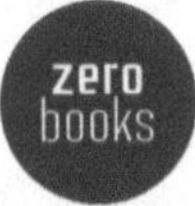

Contemporary culture has eliminated both the concept of the
public and the figure of the intellectual. Former public spaces –
both physical and cultural – are now either derelict or colonized
by advertising. A cretinous anti-intellectualism presides,
cheerled by expensively educated hacks in the pay of
multinational corporations who reassure their bored readers
that there is no need to rouse themselves from their interpassive
stupor. The informal censorship internalized and propagated by
the cultural workers of late capitalism generates a banal
conformity that the propaganda chiefs of Stalinism could only
ever have dreamt of imposing. Zer0 Books knows that another
kind of discourse – intellectual without being academic, popular
without being populist – is not only possible: it is already
flourishing, in the regions beyond the striplit malls of so-called
mass media and the neurotically bureaucratic halls of the
academy. Zer0 is committed to the idea of publishing as a
making public of the intellectual. It is convinced that in
the unthinking, blandly consensual culture in which we live,
critical and engaged theoretical reflection is more important
than ever before.